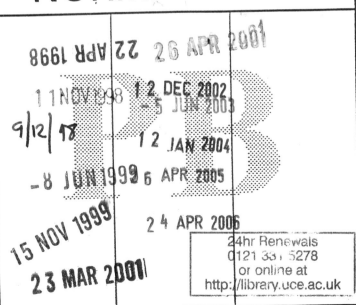

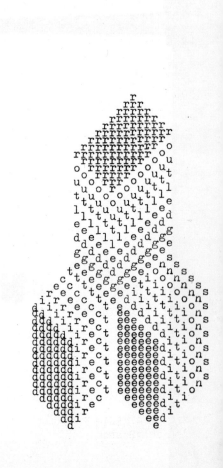

THE USE OF IMPRISONMENT
Essays in the changing state of English penal policy

Edited by
SEÁN McCONVILLE
School of Cultural and Community Studies
University of Sussex

ROUTLEDGE DIRECT EDITIONS

ROUTLEDGE & KEGAN PAUL
London and Boston

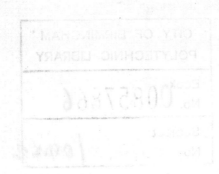

First published in 1975
by Routledge & Kegan Paul Ltd
Broadway House, 68-74 Carter Lane,
London EC4V 5EL and
9 Park Street,
Boston, Mass. 02108, USA
Typed by Molly Cooper
Printed and bound in Great Britain
by Unwin Brothers Limited,
The Gresham Press, Old Woking, Surrey
A member of the Staples Printing Group
© Routledge & Kegan Paul Ltd 1975

ISBN 0 7100 8309 2

CONTENTS

NOTES ON CONTRIBUTORS   vii

ACKNOWLEDGMENTS   ix

INTRODUCTION   xi

1   PRISONERS AND THE LAW   1
Graham Zellick

2   ADMINISTRATION: STAFF STRUCTURE AND TRAINING TODAY   17
Norman Jepson

3   ASPECTS OF THE PSYCHOLOGY OF IMPRISONMENT   32
Mark Williams

4   THE IMPRISONMENT OF FEMALES   43
Frances Heidensohn

5   CUSTODIAL ALTERNATIVES   57
Hugh J. Klare

6   ALTERNATIVES TO IMPRISONMENT   67
Keith Hawkins

7   TACTICS OF REFORM   88
Martin Wright

8   FUTURE PROSPECTS OF IMPRISONMENT IN BRITAIN   107
Seán McConville

SUGGESTED FURTHER READING   126

NOTES ON CONTRIBUTORS

KEITH HAWKINS
Fellow of Wolfson College, Oxford. Research Fellow, SSRC Centre for Socio-Legal Studies, Oxford.

FRANCES HEIDENSOHN
Lecturer in Social Policy, Civil Service College, London. Formerly Lecturer in Sociology, London School of Economics.

NORMAN JEPSON
Professor of Adult Education, University of Leeds. Adviser on Studies, Prison Staff College, Wakefield, 1962-70.

HUGH J. KLARE
Member, Board of Visitors, Long Lartin Prison and Gloucestershire Probation and After-Care Committee. Secretary, Howard League for Penal Reform, 1950-71.

SEÁN McCONVILLE
Lecturer in Social Administration, School of Cultural and Community Studies, University of Sussex.

MARK WILLIAMS
Principal Psychologist, HM Prison, Wormwood Scrubs.

MARTIN WRIGHT
Director, Howard League for Penal Reform. Formerly Librarian, Institute of Criminology, Cambridge.

GRAHAM ZELLICK
Lecturer in Laws, Queen Mary College, University of London. Visiting Professor of Law, University of Toronto.

ACKNOWLEDGMENTS

So many colleagues, students and friends have assisted in the production of this book that I cannot list them all. Margaret Guy and Janet Annis, in the initial and final stages respectively, gave willing and efficient secretarial assistance. Roger Hood and William Guinan kindly read an earlier draft, at short notice, and made some valuable suggestions. Sylvia Argyle gave generously of her time when it was needed most. To these, and to all that I have not named, my sincere thanks.

SMcC

INTRODUCTION

The theme of this collection of essays is the changing state of
English penal policy. Administrative, organizational, staffing,
legal and philosophical aspects of the present state of prisons are
examined as the contributors variously attempt to assess the reasons
for and direction of change. Although there is a general theme, and
a good deal of agreement upon issues which are raised in the essays,
there has been no attempt to reach unanimity. On a few central
issues of policy and interpretation disagreements will be evident.
Hopefully, however, any collective approach to penal policy should
find an element of diversity a strength rather than a weakness.

In different ways the majority of the articles emphasize the
failure of the treatment model of imprisonment, and note or even
support the shift from rehabilitative aims, to the objective of
'humane containment'. Various implications of this development are
examined, but it is acknowledged that many possible consequences may
still be unrecognized. Consideration of social and penal policy
cannot but bring an awareness of the very mixed motives and pressures in its formulation and the inevitable appearance of quite un-
intended effects.

The contributors differ, I suspect, in their reactions to the
present ideological impasse in penal policy; some would wear the
mantle of scepticism more easily than others. But scepticism is a
powerful common thread in the essays and an indispensable asset when
new departures are being considered.

It is too easy to forget past policy tribulations and to opt for
new global solutions. What 'treatment' was to the majority of
prison reformers in the 1950s and 1960s, 'community' may be in the
1970s. Even highly experienced commentators may be blinded to some
dangers of the 'community' prefix. Louis Blom-Cooper, in his
editorial introduction to 'Progress in Penal Reform', well exempli-
fies this when he writes: 'As a cautionary note, it is jumping to
conclusions in the other direction to take it for granted that
community treatment will always be more effective; but it is no
more ineffective, and probably has less harmful side effects.'

The cautionary note has an ironic tone. It takes little imagination to itemize many possible side-effects that may flow from a
strategic shift of formal penal measures from behind prison walls

into the community. In a world where individual liberties seem increasingly circumscribed by executive authority, the prison walls may function in some respects as an effective and desirable demarcation point for certain types of authority relations and surveillance. Indeed, it is not too far-fetched to envisage an introduction similar to this, but written a generation hence, commending the concentration rather than dispersal of measures of social control.

This collection is intended primarily for students in the social sciences, law, and professional social work training. It was originally intended to combine the essays with an extensive selection of historical and contemporary documents dealing with penal policy and prison experience. The very considerable rises in publishing costs have necessitated that this plan for a single comprehensive volume be abandoned. Instead it is hoped that a separate volume of prison readings will shortly be produced, providing, in combination with these essays, a thorough introduction to imprisonment in England. Needless to say, however, this collection and its companion may be read quite independently.

University of Sussex   Seán McConville

Chapter 1

PRISONERS AND THE LAW

Graham Zellick

The legal aspects of imprisonment in Britain have largely been
ignored. They certainly have received no systematic, let alone
critical, treatment. Orthodox penology has focused elsewhere, and
even penal reformers have until very recently had little idea what
the expression 'prisoners' rights' connoted. In the United States,
however, with a Bill of Rights at hand, the attention of lawyers
and the courts has been engaged to introduce minimum constitutional
standards of treatment into the penal systems. Prisoners' rights
has thus become a legally significant notion. In Britain, on the
other hand, the law for most purposes tends to stop at the prison
gates, leaving the prisoner to the almost exclusive control of the
prison authorities. The purpose of this chapter is to explore some
of the rights available to adult prisoners in Britain and the system within which they operate. The courts' attitude will be explained; and the institutional and legal structure of the prison
system will be briefly described. There will then follow discussions on the prisoner's access to lawyers and the courts, complaints machinery, disciplinary procedures and communication with
the outside world.

STRUCTURE AND RULES

The English penal system is the responsibility of the Home Office,
which has a separate Prison Department under the control of a senior
civil servant, the Director-General of the Prison Service, who is
also chairman of the Prison Board. Until 1963, prisons were run by
the Prison Commissioners, a semi-autonomous body, but the Home Secretary was anxious to be and appear to be in complete control of the
prison system, and to integrate the administration of prisons with
that of the probation and after-care service, which has always been
a direct Home Office responsibility. (1) The Scottish system is
distinct from the English and is covered by separate though similar
legislation. (2) It falls under the aegis of the Scottish Home and
Health Department and is the responsibility of the Secretary of
State for Scotland.
　　All penal institutions owe their existence to statute. The

principal statute for prisons is the Prison Act 1952 which lays down
the broad patterns. It has little to say on their day to day running or on the nature of the internal regime. Instead, it empowers
the Home Secretary to make rules by statutory instrument 'for the
regulation and management of prisons...and for the classification,
treatment, employment, discipline and control of persons required to
be detained therein'. (3) The principal rules are the Prison Rules
1964 (as amended). (4) A debate on the rules may take place, especially if the Opposition use their own time, as happened in 1964,
(5) and they can be annulled by a resolution of either House, although they cannot be amended. (6)

   Even the Prison Rules, however, only delineate the framework.
They prescribe certain minimum standards, confer a few rights,
impose duties, allocate responsibilities, but their striking feature
is the discretion conferred (notionally) on the Home Secretary as to
nearly all matters excepting a prisoner's right to food, clothes,
shelter and medical treatment. Because the prison system is so
large an organization, with a staff of about 20,000 and an inmate
population of almost twice that size, that discretion cannot be
delegated to officials and staff without clear guidance. Consequently, the Home Office formulates a volume of Standing Orders,
which in turn is elaborated by circular instructions and other
documents, to lay down the detailed application of the rules. But
neither the orders nor the instructions are available to anyone outside the prison service - and certainly not to prisoners. Indeed,
prisoners do not even have a right to see the Prison Rules themselves, although they are statutory instruments. Instead,
prisoners are given a Home Office summary of those parts of the
rules thought to be applicable to them. (7) This contrasts
strikingly with their right under the rules to have religious
books. (8)

   The general secrecy surrounding prisons is extremely unfortunate
and by no means essential. The Official Secrets Act silences all
those who work in prisons; and civil service rules ensure that the
personal views of Home Office officials remain unknown. This
situation is not a healthy one for the penal system. The Fulton
report on the civil service urged greater openness in government
generally; (9) and the Franks committee on the Official Secrets
Act recognized the public's right to know about prison treatment.
Their proposed Official Information Act would proscribe information
only if it were of direct use in escaping from prison. (10)

THE PRISONER AND THE LAW

The Forfeiture Act 1870 abolished the forfeiture of a felon's land
and goods, but maintained various other public disabilities for
persons convicted of treason or felony and sentenced to penal servitude, or imprisonment for twelve months or more. (11) They could
not serve in the forces, hold office under the Crown, occupy any
ecclesiastical benefice, be a member of either House of Parliament,
or vote; nor were they entitled to any public pension arising from
such service. (12) In 1965 the Criminal Law Revision Committee
recommended the abolition of the distinction between felonies and

certain things can't do if convicted.

misdemeanours. They recognized that the disabilities in the 1870
Act would lapse but felt that it was unnecessary to preserve them in
relation to any offences, especially as there were no corresponding
provisions in Scotland. (13) The Criminal Law Act 1967 enacted the
committee's recommendation, with the result that such disabilities
no longer arise, except that in 1969 all convicted prisoners were
disenfranchised for the duration of their sentences, (14) thus
extending the 1870 disability from some felons to all convicted
prisoners.

The Act of 1870 also imposed severe disabilities of a private law
nature on all those sentenced to penal servitude for felony. They
were disabled from suing, disposing or mortgaging any property, or
making any contract while serving their sentences; and their
property was vested in an administrator. This amounted to a virtual
denial of their legal personality and certainly left them without
the barest civil rights, but the disabilities were all swept away in
1948, (15) whereas the public disabilities were to survive for
another two decades.

A prisoner has always been able to make a will, as the incapacity
ceases at death; he can also be an executor of someone else's will
or an administrator under an intestacy; he can remain a trustee,
although the court has power to replace him; (16) and he can remain
a company director unless restrained by order of a court following
conviction for an offence of fraud relating to a company. (17)
In almost all respects, therefore, a convicted prisoner has the
same civil rights as the ordinary citizen, although the extent to
which he can actually exercise them will depend on the prison
authorities. He can, however, grant a power of attorney to someone
to overcome this difficulty.

Some restrictions arise even after release from prison, in
relation to serving on juries (18) and possessing firearms, (19)
for example, but there are no general disabilities.

Within prison, the ordinary law operates, so that a prisoner is
generally protected against all ordinary crimes and torts: he can
sue or prosecute in respect, for example, of injuries sustained in
prison (subject to what is said below in the section on Access to
Lawyers and Courts) as if they occurred outside. (20) The forcible
feeding of a prisoner on hunger strike is a possible exception to
this, but its legality remains to be authoritatively decided by the
courts. (21) The Home Secretary has made it clear that neither the
prison rules nor prison discipline require the forced feeding of a
prisoner on hunger strike if his capacity for rational judgment is
unimpaired, which leaves decisions in the hands of individual
medical officers. Equally, he can be made the defendant in legal
proceedings arising out of an incident in prison or otherwise. But
it is the special laws applying to prisoners that really count here;
yet the courts have held that, however worded, neither the Prison
Act nor the Prison Rules confer rights on a prisoner in the vital
sense that if they are denied he can bring a legal action either to
claim the right or compensation; and this is so even if he has
suffered damage as a result of the denial. (22) The courts' reluc-
tance to take their jurisdiction into prisons is by no means
inevitable, as the American experience has shown. Reliance on the
benevolence of public authorities has not been the typical judicial

attitude in Britain. The prisoner is robbed of the law's full
protection because the courts have been more solicitous of the problems of the prison administration than of the inmates in their care.
Yet prisoners, like all inmates of 'total institutions', are especially vulnerable and in need of greater, rather than less, legal
protection.

ACCESS TO LAWYERS AND COURTS

Yet even where the law is theoretically available to a prisoner, any
attempt to assert his legal rights will be fraught with difficulties.
This is chiefly because, under the present rules, no prisoner may
even consult a solicitor, let alone initiate proceedings, without
the Home Secretary's permission, (23) which is certainly not auto-
matic, except where a prisoner is serving a sentence of a year or
more and wishes to institute matrimonial proceedings. Often, the
Home Office will be the potential defendant, yet they still insist
on seeing the prisoner's evidence and assessing his case.
Following a complaint to the European Commission of Human Rights,
(24) the Home Office modified their practice (though not the rule)
so that permission would in future be given in cases of physical
injury alleged to be the result of the prison authorities' medical
negligence, (25) although evidence of the injury must be submitted
to the Home Office before leave is given. A House of Commons Select
Committee's suggestion of independent machinery to deal with applications to sue the Home Office (26) was rejected.
    This concession, however, was a narrow one, limited as it was to
physical injury caused by medical malpractice, and it was only a
matter of time before the restrictions were again challenged in the
European Commission, and this eventually happened in the Golder
case, the first case against Britain to have reached the European
Court of Human Rights, where it was finally decided in February
1975. (27)
    Golder was refused permission to sue a prison officer for libel.
He petitioned the European Commission, claiming that the rule
infringed two provisions in the European Convention on Human
Rights: the first spoke of the right to have legal rights and
obligations determined within a reasonable time in the ordinary
courts; the second guaranteed respect for correspondence. (28)
The United Kingdom government argued, inter alia, that the first
provision merely guaranteed basic procedural standards once a case
had reached the courts, and did not guarantee a right of access;
but even if it did, it was legitimate to prevent a prisoner from
suing if he could do so after release from prison. With regard to
correspondence, the government contended that prison authorities
must have a wide margin of discretion, which authorized the reading
and stopping of letters, even to lawyers. The Commission unanimously disagreed with these contentions and, friendly settlement
having failed, the government referred the case to the Court. By a
majority, the Court held that the first of the provisions in the
Convention did confer a right of access to the courts, which the
prison rule infringed, even where it merely delayed the institution
of proceedings until the prisoner's discharge; and the Court

further held, this time unanimously, that the rule also violated the right of respect for correspondence.

As a result, the Prison Rules must be amended in order to maintain conformity with the Convention, and the Home Office have this in hand at the present time. It is clear that prisoners must be allowed to institute proceedings if they wish and to communicate with lawyers with a view to doing so. What remains unclear from the Court's judgment is how far letters to solicitors, and indeed letters generally, must be freed from censorship and control as a result of the Court's unanimous decision concerning correspondence. Although the relevant provision does permit qualifications on the right to correspond - where, for example, it is 'necessary in a democratic society in the interests of...public safety..., for the prevention of disorder or crime...or for the protection of the rights and freedoms of others' - the Court has failed to make clear whether every particular act of interference with a prisoner's correspondence must be justifiable on one of these grounds, or whether limitations may be imposed generally on these grounds. All that can be observed now is that if the amended rules interpret the judgment narrowly, the issue will again find its way to Strasbourg in due course for an authoritative ruling.

The Home Office has always taken the view that because many prisoners are disaffected, frustrated and bored, large numbers of frivolous and groundless actions would be brought against them if restrictions were abandoned. What this ignores, however, is not only the advice which many lawyers would give that there was no basis for a case, but, more importantly, the fact that nearly all prisoners, however litigious, would require legal aid, which is given only where the legal aid committee is satisfied that the plaintiff has an arguable case. He has no right to argue the case in person, and cannot therefore secure his release from prison to do so. (29)

Even apart from the restrictions imposed by the rules, the practical difficulties of obtaining legal advice are formidable, since lawyers are not readily available. Despite the '£25 Scheme' introduced in 1972, (30) whereby up to £25 worth of legal advice and assistance is available from a solicitor to those with low incomes, including prisoners, contact with lawyers remains difficult: lawyers are reluctant to visit prisons, often situated in remote places, so that a prisoner will never conveniently and simply be able to receive skilled advice on the many domestic and other problems likely to trouble him. This is soluble only by a programme of regular visits to prisons by independent lawyers, as in some American states and Ontario, which would reduce prisoners' anxieties, lessen tension, and maintain all-important contacts with the outside world.

Once a prisoner becomes a party to legal proceedings - either because leave has been given to sue, or he is being prosecuted for another offence, or sued, or is an appellant or remand prisoner awaiting trial - the Prison Rules provide special facilities for writing to and seeing legal advisers. (31) Special permission is, however, needed actually to attend the court hearing, even under escort. (32)

The absence of independent legal advice is also significant in the context of prison disciplinary procedures, clearly of critical importance in any 'total institution' with a strictly controlled regime.   This aspect will be considered in a separate section below.

COMPLAINTS

The opportunities open to a prisoner to ventilate grievances, so important in a disciplined environment in which contact with those outside is controlled, appear extensive on paper.   It is convenient to distinguish between the formal internal machinery and the opportunities to raise complaints with those outside the prison system, both official and unofficial.

The internal opportunities range from the governor, through the board of visitors (described below) to the Home Secretary.   'Every request by a prisoner', state the rules, (33) 'to see the governor, a visiting officer of the Secretary of State or a member of the board of visitors shall be recorded by the officer to whom it is made and promptly passed on to the governor'.   A similar provision applies to the medical officer. (34)   The governor (or his deputy) is required to hear prisoners' applications on every day other than Sunday. (35)   A request to see a member of the board or visiting officer of the Home Secretary is to be passed to that person on his next visit to the prison. (36)

Every prison has a board of visitors. (37)   Until 1971, local prisons had 'visiting committees' instead of boards of visitors. (38)   These were composed of local magistrates appointed to the committee by the local quarter sessions - in effect by all the local magistrates - the last vestige of the administration of prisons by local government. (39)   Members of boards are appointed by the Home Secretary, about half being magistrates.   (Board members are not to be confused with 'prison visitors', who are volunteers authorized by the Home Secretary to befriend prisoners with whom they are not otherwise acquainted.)   They are required to meet at the prison at least once a month, with two main duties: (40)   to 'satisfy themselves as to the state of the prison premises, the administration of the prison and the treatment of the prisoners', with a power to suspend any officer if necessary;   and to adjudicate on the more serious disciplinary offences (described in the next section).   The board is further required to 'hear any complaint or request which a prisoner wishes to make';   to inspect the food at frequent intervals;   and to arrange a rota whereby at least one member visits the prison between each meeting.   In particular, a member has access to every part of the prison and to every prisoner at any time;   he has access to the prison records;   and may interview any prisoner in complete privacy.   This power of entry to prisons and access to prisoners extends to every magistrate in respect of the prisons in his area, but it is little-used. (41)

These are considerable powers possessed by the board but in practice they prove less extensive.   First, so many of the important decisions are for the Home Office - for example, transfer to another prison - that all the board can do is make a recommendation.   They may, however, grant extra visits or letters, for example. (42)

Second, many of the real complaints about imprisonment - living conditions, diet, overcrowding, type of work, educational facilities - are wholly beyond the scope of the board. Third, prisoners have little confidence in the boards, which they come to identify with the management of the prison, a factor all the more understandable when it is remembered that boards are also the principal disciplinary tribunal. That is not to say, however, that the board of visitors is not a valuable feature of the English prison system. It does suggest, though, that reform is necessary, at least to separate the board's two incompatible functions so that it might enjoy rather more confidence among prisoners than at present.

Finally, a prisoner is entitled to petition the Home Secretary on any matter. This prisoners do in large numbers, which means of course that many will get no further than a relatively junior Prison Department official. The petition will be sent from the prison together with the governor's comments. No hearing or interview will take place, and it may take many months before an answer is received. The answer will rarely give reasons and is in purely formal terms.

Significantly restraining the making of complaints are two disciplinary offences created by the Prison Rules: 'making any false and malicious allegation against an officer' and 'repeatedly making groundless complaints'. (43) A prisoner who finds his complaint disbelieved, because he has insufficient proof or his word is suspect, may find himself the subject of disciplinary proceedings for having persisted in his complaint. This to a large extent vitiates the internal machinery for ventilating grievances, but there is a genuine dilemma here, for the interests of the prison staff cannot properly be ignored. They deserve some protection against malicious or groundless allegations, although the appropriate device for affording that protection is not easy to discover.

Prisoners, therefore, have ample opportunities to make known their individual grievances within the prison system, but very rarely will it result in any positive action. Sometimes, of course, it will and it is not suggested that there would be any advantage in curtailing existing provisions in this respect. It does mean, though, that a prisoner will think also of communicating his grievance to some person or body outside the prison system - that is, to an independent source - for investigation or action. Opportunities to speak collectively are non-existent in most prisons, although the Home Secretary is seeking ways of improving this - short of recognizing a prisoners' union. (44) The distinction here is between organization within particular institutions and across institutions, the latter being anathema. Because prisoners are effectively isolated from the community, access to outside bodies is essential. These may be official - members of Parliament, the Parliamentary Commissioner (or 'Ombudsman'), the European Commission of Human Rights - or unofficial - the press, the Howard League, the National Council for Civil Liberties, Justice, PROP. This last category will be discussed in the section on letters.

The Parliamentary Commissioner for Administration's jurisdiction extends to prisons, (45) and a number of prisoners' complaints have reached him. In one case, mentioned above, he invited the Home Office to 'review' the rule which prohibits a prisoner from suing the Home Office without their permission. The 'review' accordingly took place and the rule was found to be satisfactory! (46) The discretion in prison administration is so wide and loose that unless a decision is unmistakably marked by perversity, bias or delay, a prisoner's prospects with the Commissioner are poor.

Cases reach the Commissioner only through members of Parliament and, surprisingly though it may seem, prisoners have no unrestricted right to contact their constituency member. They are required first to have exhausted all internal methods, which usually will take several months, by which time the sentence may have been served. Correspondence between a prisoner and his member will be read by the prison authorities in the usual way; and a visit will usually be allowed. This of course raises the whole question of letters and visits, which will be considered in the next section. Suffice it to say for now that a prisoner will never be allowed to write to the press.

The remaining official avenue open to a prisoner is the European Commission of Human Rights in Strasbourg. In 1966, the British Government, already a signatory to the European Convention on Human Rights, granted the optional right of individual petition, whereby individuals may bring actions against governments alleging violations of the rights guaranteed under the Convention. A consequence of granting the right of individual petition is that no impediments to the effective exercise of the right are permitted. A prisoner thus has an absolute right to petition and communicate with the Commission. This is not accorded by the Prison Rules but is accepted by the prison authorities. It is ironic that a prisoner has freer access to the Commission in Strasbourg than to any English court which requires leave of the Home Secretary. A prisoner must first have exhausted all domestic remedies and must then satisfy the Commission that his case is admissible. If it is, a hearing will be arranged, and legal aid may be granted by the Commission. If there is no 'friendly settlement' and the Commission's view is adverse to the government, the matter will be resolved either by the Committee of Ministers or the European Court of Human Rights. The singular advantage of this machinery is that a challenge may be made, not just to the actual decision or exercise of discretion, nor even to an administrative practice and regulation on which it is based, but to the actual statutory provision concerned. This is akin to the role of the American courts in applying the Bill of Rights to shape prison reform, although thus far the European Commission has been less vigorous and creative in its approach than many American courts, with the general practice among European states representing the minimum standards which the Commission will enforce. However, the European Commission may well have a significant impact on prisoners' rights in this country in the course of time, and the decision of the European Court in the Golder case confirms the far-reaching implications of the Convention.

LETTERS AND VISITS

Such is the prisoner's position that the maintenance of contact with the outside world is vital if he is to return to the community on release and lead a normal life. It is also important in the context of grievances already considered. Yet the one subject a prisoner is not allowed to write about, although this is not always strictly enforced, is his prison conditions, an extraordinary proscription with little justification. He is, however, allowed to write to organizations like the National Council for Civil Liberties about his case. Not only is there censorship of all mail, (47) incoming and outgoing, but the number of letters he may write is limited. Again, the Home Secretary's discretion is extensive, but the rules do allow a prisoner to write and receive one letter a week, of reasonable length, (48) but this minimum is usually exceeded by 'canteen letters', the postage being paid by the prisoner. The rules permit him one visit every month in the sight and hearing of an officer, (49) although this minimum is exceeded in some establishments. Remand prisoners are entitled to write any number of letters and receive daily visits, (50) but these are usually 'closed visits' in which the visitor is separated from the prisoner by a glass screen. Until recently, appellants were entitled to unlimited visits from anyone, wives included, in connection with their appeals, but such visits are now confined to their legal advisers on the false assumption that all appellants are adequately advised by lawyers. (51) No prisoner is currently allowed access to a telephone, but experiments with remand prisoners are to be tried. Conjugal visits are not permitted, but home leave towards the end of a sentence is sometimes allowed and is to be extended.

But why censorship? It is a great burden on prison staff to have to read, albeit superficially, every letter to and from a prisoner. It may take up all the time of as many as three prison officers in a medium-sized prison. The irony is that this burden is then used to justify a restriction on the number and length of letters a prisoner may write! The rationale of censorship seems to be as follows: to prevent arrangements to facilitate escape; to prevent crimes being planned that might be implemented either during a sentence or after discharge from prison; to acquaint the prison authorities with any social or domestic problems which might affect a prisoner; and to prevent the smuggling of contraband - money, drugs, tobacco and alcohol.

Yet the list of restrictions goes considerably beyond what these reasons could possibly support by proscribing, for example, any reference to prison conditions or even communication with a marriage bureau. (52) It is obvious that it is unnecessary to read letters in order to discover contraband. As for arranging escapes or crimes, it is well known that prisoners experience few difficulties in conveying messages, even letters, to those outside if they are determined enough. In any event, it is scarcely likely that prisoners will entrust such matters to the post. That leaves concern for the prisoner's personal problems - a paternalistic attitude which cannot be reconciled with the prisoner's right to privacy. Experiments abandoning censorship are now taking place in a few establishments (53) and they may lead to the complete

abolition of the practice when the Home Office discovers that the
anticipated chaos and disruption does not materialize. In any
event, the rules relating to letters will probably undergo some
changes when the amendments to the rules following the Golder case
in the European Court of Human Rights are introduced.

DISCIPLINARY PROCEDURES

In addition to the operation in prisons of the ordinary criminal
law, which includes a number of offences relating specifically to
prisons, like escape, rescue or smuggling contraband, (54) the
Prison Rules create a number of offences against discipline, some
of which are also criminal offences. These fall into three categories: 'especially grave offences' are mutiny, incitement to
mutiny and doing gross personal violence to an officer; (55)
'graver offences' are escaping or attempting to escape, assaulting
an officer and doing gross personal violence to anyone else; (56)
the remaining seventeen offences are less serious and include
assault; absenting oneself from any place where one is required to
be; having any unauthorized article; stealing; damaging property;
making a false and malicious allegation against an officer;
treating an officer or any person visiting a prison with disrespect;
using abusive, insolent, threatening or other improper language;
being indecent in language, act or gesture; repeatedly making
groundless complaints; being idle, careless or negligent at work;
disobeying any lawful order or prison rule or regulation; attempting to do any of these things; and in any way offending against
good order and discipline. (57)
Not only are these offences broad in scope, but some are so
lacking in specificity as to invite abuse and be open to criticism.
More serious criticism can be levelled at the procedures for
dealing with offences.
It is clear from the above list that almost all criminal offences
will also be offences against discipline. Whether a crime will be
dealt with by the ordinary courts or the internal disciplinary
machinery is in practice a matter for the prison authorities. It is
possible for both to take place without offending the rule against
double jeopardy. (58) Very serious offences like murder will
invariably be dealt with by the courts, but grave crimes like
grievous bodily harm may nevertheless be disposed of internally,
while less serious matters may end up in the courts if, for example,
the prison authorities are anxious to show a firm resolve in dealing
with prison disturbances. A charge of riot may result, as it did
after the Parkhurst disturbances in 1969, in lengthy prison
sentences, a much harsher penalty than could have been imposed by
the board of visitors. Another factor which may influence the
decision is the quality of the evidence, since it will in practice
be more difficult to secure a conviction in the Crown Court before
a jury than before the board of visitors.
Offences against discipline will be dealt with either by the
governor or the board of visitors, the board dealing with the
'graver offences' and the 'especially grave offences' and the
governor dealing with the rest unless he thinks it is serious enough

to be referred to the board, since the board can award more severe
penalties. The governor may caution, order loss of privileges for
up to 28 days, exclusion from associated work for up to 14 days,
stoppage of earnings for up to 28 days, cellular (that is, solitary)
confinement for up to three days, and loss of remission of sentence
of up to 28 days. (59) The board may caution, order loss of privileges for any period, exclusion from associated work for up to 56
days, stoppage of earnings for up to 56 days, cellular confinement
for up to 56 days, and loss of remission of up to 180 days, (60) or
longer in the case of the 'especially grave offences'. (61)
Corporal punishment, which could be awarded for 'especially grave
offencies', was abolished in 1967 (62) and bread-and-water punishment in 1974. (63) Awards may now be suspended (64) and remission
once lost may be restored, (65) both of which serve as inducements
to subsequent good behaviour.

These awards, especially those available to the board, are
certainly severe. Solitary confinement for two months or loss of
remission of six months, which is equivalent to a nine months'
prison sentence with three months' remission, are obviously harsh
sanctions. Moreover, these are the awards that may be made in
respect of each offence, so that a board may make several awards
involving, say, loss of remission which in total are considerably
in excess of 180 days. Every prisoner serving more than a month's
imprisonment is entitled to remission of one-third of his sentence
'on the ground of his industry and good conduct'. (66) Remission
will in practice be lost only by order of the governor or board for
a distinct offence, but the Home Secretary may in his discretion
refuse to grant remission. (67) Calculation of the time served
includes any period spent in prison awaiting trial (68) and remission is now calculated on the entire sentence. (69) It may
accordingly be forfeited in respect of a remand prisoner who has
misbehaved even before he has been convicted or sentenced. (70)
Parole is distinct from remission, having been introduced in 1967,
and is entirely discretionary, the decision being made by the Home
Secretary on the recommendation of the Parole Board or, in some
cases, by the local review committee. (71) Parole may be given
after one-third of a sentence has been served, provided that the
prisoner has been in prison for a year. A paroled prisoner is
released on licence and may be recalled. Although parole is not
expressly affected by decisions of the governor or board, infrac-
tions of the rules will inevitably have a bearing on a prisoner's
application. Another unexpressed sanction available to the prison
authorities is transfer to another prison, over which a prisoner
has no control. Rule 43 should also be mentioned in this connection
since it authorizes the governor to remove a prisoner 'from
association' - that is, segregate him from other prisoners - 'Where
it appears desirable, for the maintenance of good order or discipline or in (the prisoner's) interests ...either generally or for
particular purposes'. The authority of a member of the board or of
the Home Secretary is required if the segregation is to exceed 24
hours. Each order lasts for a month, but may be renewed any number
of times.

In view of the boards' extensive powers, the procedures for
dealing with offences are of great importance. The Home Secretary

is required to make rules 'for ensuring that a person who is charged with any offence under the rules shall be given a proper opportunity of presenting his case', (72) but the rules are far from extensive. A prisoner 'on report' is to be informed of the charge as soon as possible. This will be done in writing. The governor will inquire into the matter within 24 hours and either dispose of the case or refer it to the board. (73) As to the procedure, the rules state simply that the 'prisoner shall be given a full opportunity of hearing what is alleged against him and of presenting his own case'. (74)

Despite the severity of the sentences that may be imposed, whether it is a governor's adjudication or a board's, the hearing will be private; there will be no legally-trained person to advise either the governor or the board members on the law or procedure; there is no formal appeal apart from petitioning the Home Secretary; and neither legal assistance (75) nor a friend at one's side is permitted. Furthermore, the governor is present at the board's hearing, and so are a number of prison officers; the prisoner will be uneasy and possibly intimidated; it will very likely be his word against an officer's; and the right to call witnesses is largely illusory, since other inmates will be reluctant to expose themselves to possible victimization later whether by staff or other inmates. Also, the prisoner may have been in solitary confinement since the charge was preferred, (76) making the preparation of his defence almost impossible. Moreover, many prisoners have a low intellectual ability, poor education and inadequate verbal powers. In any event, both calling witnesses and cross-examining require the chairman's or governor's permission, and questions in cross-examination have to be put through the chairman or governor.

These features of the system of dealing with disciplinary offences are disquieting and fall seriously below the normal standards of natural justice to be found in courts or tribunals. The subject was last investigated by an official committee in 1951, which was generally satisfied with the system as it stood. (77)

Possibilities for fundamental reform include a right to elect trial before the ordinary courts if the charge discloses a criminal offence, at least of a certain level of seriousness, and alterations to the procedure of the boards so that it at least conforms to the standards of a magistrates' court, with a right to legal representation and a formal appeal system. A new disciplinary body would be necessary, possibly composed exclusively of magistrates but chaired by a lawyer, if the dual functions of supervision and discipline presently exercised by boards of visitors were discontinued, leaving boards their supervisory function only. A different tribunal to deal with these matters is the principal recommendation of the Jellicoe committee on boards of visitors, set up by Justice, the Howard League and NACRO. (78)

CONCLUSION

The two striking features of the issues curveyed in this chapter are first, the general lack of interest in them and second, the absence of intervention by the courts and even Parliament, leaving so much to the discretion of the Home Office in contradistinction to the elaborate legal safeguards that operate until conviction. Happily, the former is changing: the latter remains as true now as ever it did.

Clearly, a sentence of imprisonment must inevitably involve a loss of certain rights. How far a prisoner's rights merit restriction is something demanding constant appraisal. If the statements of principle with which the Prison Rules open are to be meaningful, re-examination of many aspects of prison life, leading to new Prison Rules, is overdue. The first two rules deserve quoting:

> 1 The purpose of the training and treatment of convicted prisoners shall be to encourage and assist them to lead a good and useful life.
> 2 - (1) Order and discipline shall be maintained with firmness, but with no more restriction than is required for safe custody and well ordered community life....
> (3) At all times the treatment of prisoners shall be such as to encourage their self-respect and a sense of personal responsibility....

There have undoubtedly been great improvements this century in food, clothing, the relationship between inmates and officers, the abolition of the silence rule, opportunities for association and much else. But in so many respects the legal position of the prisoner remains primitive. Unlike the rest of us, the prisoner may not infer that he can do whatever is not expressly prohibited. His every action is regulated. The rules are nearly always apt for the purpose. And even where rights are conferred - like the remand prisoner's right to have food sent in (79) - it is often difficult to exercise them.

Prisoners are very rarely given reasons for decisions that affect them, however directly. The effect on a person of being thus treated cannot be exaggerated. It is scarcely consistent with rules 1 and 2 just cited. It does nothing to rehabilitate him, to make him better able to rejoin society on release. The essential point is that every prisoner finds his dignity and self-respect diminished. The purpose of this is obscure. Possibly it is unintentional. But if imprisonment is ever to prove more successful than it has been, and to do less damage to those in its care, a new regime should be introduced, with a fresh conception of the prisoner. Not all will respond, but some will and that is enough. It is in society's interest, too, and not just the prisoners'. The guiding principle might be that the only rights to be lost on imprisonment are those that are necessarily and inevitably lost as a consequence of that imprisonment. Gratuitous denial of legal and civic rights is as anachronistic, and as fruitless, as the widespread imprisonment of debtors, long since abolished.

NOTES

(Sections and rules not otherwise identified are references to the Prison Act 1952 and the Prison Rules 1964 (as amended) respectively.)

1   The Prison Commissioners Dissolution Order 1963 (S.I. 1963 No. 597); Criminal Justice Act 1961, s. 24.

2 Prisons (Scotland) Act 1952.
3 s. 47.
4 S.I. 1964 No. 388; The Prison (Amendment) Rules 1968 (S.I. 1968 No. 440), 1971 No. 2019), 1972 (S.I. 1972 No. 1860) and 1974 (S.I. 1974 No. 713).
5 687 H.C. Debs, cols 1351-1416 (23 January 1964).
6 Criminal Justice Act 1967, s. 66 (4).
7 r. 7 (1).
8 r. 16.
9 'The Civil Service' (Cmnd 3638, 1968).
10 'Report of the Departmental Committee on Section 2 of the Official Secrets Act 1911' (Cmnd 5104, 1972), paras 172 and 175.
11 'Outlawry' was finally abolished in 1938: Administration of Justice (Miscellaneous Provisions) Act 1938, s. 12.
12 Under the Criminal Justice Act 1948, s. 70 (2), the pension could be subsequently restored.
13 Seventh Report: 'Felonies and Misdemeanours' (Cmnd 2659, 1965), para. 79.
14 Representation of the People Act 1969, s. 4, implementing the recommendation of the Speaker's Conference on Electoral Law (Cmnd 3550, 1968) and the subsequent White Paper (Cmnd 3717, 1968).
15 Criminal Justice Act 1948, s. 70 (1).
16 Trustee Act 1925, s. 41 (as amended by the Criminal Law Act 1967).
17 Companies Act 1948, s. 188.
18 Criminal Justice Act 1972, s. 25 (1) and Sched. 2, Pt II.
19 Firearms Act 1968, s. 21.
20 A criminal prosecution for assault cannot be brought against the Home Secretary but it can be brought against the governor or other officers concerned: R. v. Morton Brown, ex p. Ainsworth (1910) 74 J.P. 53 (D.C.); R. v. Huggins (1730) 2 Strange 883. A case of damages being awarded against a visiting committee is noted in S. Hobhouse and Fenner Brockway, 'English Prisons Today' (1922), p.392. The Home Secretary is vicariously liable for the torts of his agents: Crown Proceedings Act 1947. The responsibility of the prison authorities to prisoners is laid down in Ellis v. Home Office (1953) 2 All E.R. 149 (C.A.).
21 877 H.C. Debs, col. 451 (17 July 1974). The only case directly on the point is Leigh v. Gladstone (1909) 26 T.L.R. 139, which held that there was a duty to force feed; but there was no legal argument, the questions really being whether excessive force had been used or whether it was necessary to force feed that prisoner, it was a first-instance decision, and suicide and attempted suicide were then crimes.
22 Arbon v. Anderson (1943) 1 K.B. 252; Hinds v. Home Office, 'The Times', 17 January 1962 (C.A.); R. v. Carlile (1822) 1 Dow. and Ry. K.B. 535.
23 r. 34 (8).
24 Knechtl v. U.K., Application No. 4115/69, 36 Coll. 43 (1971); Report of the Commission, 24 March 1972.
25 'Second Report from the Select Committee on the Parliamentary Commissioner for Administration, Session 1970-71: Observations by the Government' (Cmnd 4846, 1971).

26   'Second Report from the Select Committee on the Parliamentary
      Commissioner for Administration, Session 1970-71' (H.C. 513 of
      1971), p. xii.
27   Golder v. U.K., Application No. 4451/70, 37 Coll. 124 (1971).
      Report of the Commission, 1 June 1973; Judgment of the Court,
      21 February 1975.
28   Arts 6 and 8.
29   E.g. Weldon v. Neal (1885) 15 Q.B.D. 471.
30   Legal Aid Act 1974, s. 2, re-enacting the Legal Advice and
      Assistance Act 1972.
31   r. 37A (inserted by S.I. 1972 No. 1860, r.3).
32   Criminal Justice Act 1961, s. 29. Habeas corpus is available if
      the prisoner's testimony is necessary: Rules of the Supreme
      Court, Ord. 54, r.9. See also the Criminal Procedure Act 1853,
      s. 9.
33   r. 8 (1).
34   r. 17 (2).
35   r. 8 (2).
36   r. 8 (3).
37   s. 6 (2).
38   Courts Act 1971, s. 53 (3); S.I. 1971 No. 2019, rr. 4-5.
39   The local control of prisons was terminated by the Prison Act
      1877, which placed all prisons under central control and created
      the Prison Commissioners and visiting committees.
40   rr. 92-7.
41   s. 19 (as amended by the Local Government Act 1972, Sched. 30).
42   r. 34 (6).
43   r. 47 (12) and (16).
44   845 H.C. Debs, col. 1171 (9 November 1972).
45   Parliamentary Commissioner Act 1967, s. 4 (1) and Sched. 2.
46   'First Report of the Parliamentary Commissioner for Administra-
      tion, Session 1970-71', Annual Report for 1970 (H.C. 261 of
      1971), p. 127.
47   r. 33 (3) (as amended by S.I. 1974 No. 713, r.3).
48   r. 34 (2) (a).
49   r. 34 (2) (b) (as amended by S.I. 1974 No. 713, r. 4).
50   r. 34 (1).
51   r. 60 was revoked by S.I. 1972 No. 1860, r. 4; r. 37A (supra)
      applies instead. See Michael Zander, 'Legal Advice and Criminal
      Appeals: A Survey of Prisoners, Prisons and Lawyers' (1972)
      Crim. L.R. 132.
52   'Second Report of the Parliamentary Commissioner for Administra-
      tion, Session 1968-69', Annual Report for 1968, p.47.
53   'Report on the work of the Prison Department 1972' (Cmnd 5375,
      1973), para. 88.
54   E.g. ss. 39-41.
55   rr. 47 and 52 (as amended by S.I. 1974 No. 713).
56   rr. 47 and 51 (as amended by S.I. 1974 No. 713).
57   r. 47.
58   R. v. Hogan (1960) 2 Q.B. 513 (C.C.A.).
59   r. 50 (as amended by S.I. 1974 No. 713).
60   r. 51 (4) (as amended by S.I. 1974 No. 713).
61   r. 52 (3) (as amended by S.I. 1974 No. 713).
62   Criminal Justice Act 1967, s. 65.

63   S.I. 1974 No. 713, r. 5 and Sched., Pt II.
64   r. 55 (introduced by S.I. 1974 No. 713).
65   r. 56 (introduced by S.I. 1974 No. 713).
66   s. 25 (1);   r. 5 (as amended by S.I. 1968 No. 440, r. 1 and
     Sched.).
67   Morriss v. Winter (1929) 1 K.B. 243;   R. v. Governor of Leeds
     Prison, ex p. Stafford (1964) 2 Q.B. 625, 630 (D.C);   R. v.
     Maguire (1956) 40 Cr.App.R. 92, 94 (C.C.A.);   Hancock v. Prison
     Commissioners (1960) 1 Q.B. 117;   Re Savundra (1973) 3 All E.R.
     406.
68   Criminal Justice Act 1967, s. 67.
69   r. 5 (2) (a) (introduced by S.I. 1968 No. 440).
70   r. 54 (introduced by S.I. 1974 No. 713).
71   Criminal Justice Act 1967.
72   s. 47 (2).
73   r. 48 (3) and (4).
74   r. 49.
75   This has been confirmed by the Court of Appeal in Fraser v.
     Mudge, 'The Times', 13 June 1975.
76   r. 48 (2).
77   'Report of a Committee to Review Punishments in Prisons,
     Borstal Institutions, Approved Schools and Remand Homes', Part I
     and II: Prisons and Borstal Institutions (Cmd 8256, 1951).   At
     the time of writing a Home Office working party is examining the
     procedure at adjudications and should soon complete its task.
     The report will be published.
78   'Boards of Visitors of Penal Institutions' (1975), pp.69-71.
79   r. 21 (1).

POSTSCRIPT

While this chapter was going to press, the Home Secretary announced
the changes he was proposing to make in the Prison Rules following
the European Court's decision in the Golder case (HC Debs, 5 August
1975).   Henceforth, inmates will be allowed to seek legal advice
about taking legal proceedings, and to institute such proceedings,
without having to apply for permission, except where the proposed
proceedings concern 'the administration of establishments', in which
case the internal complaints machinery must first be used.   Access
to lawyers more generally is not to be facilitated, and the only re-
laxation in censorship will be in open prisons, where it will
largely be abandoned in respect of letters to relatives and friends.
The Home Secretary denied that the court's decision affected censorship generally, although he is reviewing the question of censorship
of correspondence with Members of Parliament.   The narrowness of
the proposed change has disappointed many observers;   and, more
significantly, it may fail to give full effect to the court's decision.

Chapter 2

ADMINISTRATION: STAFF STRUCTURE AND TRAINING TODAY

Norman Jepson

1 INCREASING SIZE AND DIVERSITY

There are now 15,000 public servants working in the prison service. Their wages and salaries in the last financial year amounted to about £24m, something over half the total cost of the prison system. Like any other service or organisation dealing with people, the prison system is therefore 'labour intensive' and it is important that staff should be of the right quality, well trained and efficiently used. (1)

a Size and central structure

One of the most significant features of the English prison service in the generation following the Second World War has been its growth in overall size and in the diversity of establishments. The White Paper 'People in Prison' recorded, 'there are now about 35,000 people in custody compared with about 20,000 in 1950....During the same period the total number of staff employed in the prison service has increased from 5,500 to 15,000....The Prison Department is now responsible for 111 institutions compared with 57 in 1950'. (2) Compared with the inter-war years the prison service has trebled in size in almost all aspects - number of inmates, staff and institutions. To appreciate the significance of this increase for the basic organization of the prison service it is necessary, however, to see it within the context of a penal system which has changed in two important respects. Ironically, although the prison service has expanded so rapidly it has come to occupy a relatively less important place in the sentencing process, as an increasing range of alternatives has been introduced and utilized. Meanwhile, some of the extreme factors which distinguished and isolated one penal method from another have been modified. On the one hand, the general characteristic of prisons that they are concerned exclusively with dealing with offenders excluded from society has been modified, with the introduction of open prisons, prison hostels, home leave and work in the community. On the other hand, the involvement of the probation service in an increasing range of activities including prison 'through-care' has blunted the image of probation as being solely concerned with treatment in the community. Prisons and probation are now treated less as polarities and more as complementary institutions. Reflecting these developments there have been three important organizational changes during the past decade aimed at integrating the prison service into a more complex penal system and integrating individual prisons within an enlarged and more diversified prison service. First, in the early 1960s, the old Prison Commission which had been responsible for the prison service centrally, was abolished and its powers vested in the Home Secretary. 'Public responsibility in respect of crime - for prevention, for treatment in institutions, and for after-care - would be brought clearly under one Department of State'. (3) Second, and somewhat later, regionalization was introduced and England and Wales were divided into four regions, each with its own Regional Director, and staff. If the abolition of the Prison Commission was symbolic of a need to integrate the different facets of penal policy, regionalization was not only a process of decentralization, but a means of reducing the isolation of one penal establishment from another. In face of growth, diversification, and increased problems of security and control, regionalization emphasized not the independence of establishments and their governors but rather their interdependence. Finally, in the 1970s, have come changes in the management structure of the Prison Department which aimed in part to bring headquarters and establishments on the one hand, and civil service and prison staff on the other, into closer touch:

> There are no longer senior posts which are the exclusive preserve of members of the administrative or executive classes of the Civil Service and others which are the preserve of those who have previously been governors of prisons and borstals. Nor are the latter seen primarily as advisers. Staff of different backgrounds and experience work as an integrated team. (4)

b Diversity and local structure

But the expansion, at least in staff and institutions, still continues. The most recent prison Department Report (1972) at the time of writing, puts the total staffing figure at nearly 19,000 and an expenditure of nearly £42m. on pay and allowances out of a total net expenditure on the prison service of some £78m. (5) While the administration, staffing and training of the prison service are affected by overall growth, they are equally affected by the increasing diversity of establishments that come within the jurisdiction of the Prison Department, as for example the remand centres and detention centres, introduced following the 1948 Criminal Justice Act, the maximum security units and prisons following in the wake of the Mountbatten Report on Security (1966) and the specialized institutions like Grendon and Coldingley reflecting respectively the emphasis upon psychiatric treatment and industrial enterprise. This diversity raises important questions about how far the structures of prison establishments at a local level reflect their specialized functions or conform to a more uniform pattern.

The official classification of penal establishments meanwhile reveals something more of this diversity and of the distribution of inmates and staff in different types of establishments (see Table 2.1). (6)

TABLE 2.1

| Type of institution | 1972 | | | | 1969 |
| | No. of institutions | | Average prison population | | Prison officers (male) |
	Male	Female	Male	Female	
Local	23	1	14,994	305	4,214
Remand centre	10	3	1,962	153	
Closed training	31	1	9,884	183	2,433
Open training	12	2	3,578	164	598
Closed borstal	13	2	3,395	141	1,518
Open borstal	12	1	1,797	34	
Senior detention	13	-	1,351	-	633
Junior detention	6	-	387	-	
			37,348	980	

Two factors stand out clearly from this system of classification, namely that whilst there is this marked diversification of establishments, the prison service, both in respect of inmates and staff, is numerically dominated by closed establishments, which claim some 80 per cent of personnel. It is also dominated by the local prisons and remand centres, which are responsible for the holding of prisoners on trial and/or awaiting sentence and which attract more than 40 per cent of all prisoners and prison staff. (7) One question that should be asked, therefore, is the extent to which within this nationalized enterprise, the structure of different institutions and their staffing and training programmes tend to be dominated by the needs of the 'local' and the 'closed'. Elsewhere, in an article entitled 'Learning and Experience', I pose this question and attempt to develop the implications more fully:

The increasing diversity of establishments gives rise to a sequence of questions relevant to staff training. Does this diversity imply that prison service personnel of similar status are performing dissimilar functions in the different institutions? If they are, are they stationed in one type of institution sufficiently long to be regarded as becoming specialists in these functions? - Is it therefore still meaningful

to speak of a general-purpose prison officer than say, a
specialist borstal officer or a specialist local prison officer?
- Does/should the training organization reflect primarily the
specialism or the generality?

Different systems of classification, such as, for example, ones
based on length of sentence and/or the mobility of the prison population would raise equally basic questions for the structure and
staffing of institutions. The classification system, however, which
has probably been examined most thoroughly and which highlights the
problem most effectively is that based on different treatment or
training methods and objectives. One example is the study by an
English sociologist aptly titled Administrative Consequences of
Penal Objectives (8) in which the writer suggests classifying penal
establishments according to four 'penal goals' - (i) Passive Deterrence; (ii) Active Deterrence; (iii) Passive Treatment;
(iv) Active Treatment. Passive Deterrence is defined thus: 'Loss
of liberty is the main deterrent device...(there is) no deliberate
attempt at individual treatment.' It might well apply to many local
prisons. Active Deterrence, meanwhile, is 'deterrence (which) is
deliberately organized' and under such a heading might be placed the
early detention centres. Passive Treatment is seen as 'constructive
facilities for work, education, leisure and welfare...but no real
attempt at individual treatment planning based on continuous con-
sultation', as compared with Active Treatment which is defined as a
situation in which 'the offender is not merely exposed to a constructive regime, he is inserted into it in a way which is most
consistent with his needs, taking into account the problem of running the institution as a whole.' The significance of these last
two categories is most aptly illustrated in a study by Bottoms and
McClintock (9) in which they analyse the transformation of a borstal
from what is virtually the Passive Treatment model to that of the
Active Treatment (and back again) with the consequent modification
of structure, role and staff training. The structure changed from
one based essentially on the 'house' and 'work' system to a more
centralized one based on the need to diagnose individual problems
and plan individual programmes, utilizing the total resources of the
institution. In turn the role of the officer became more treatment-
rather than training-orientated whilst the role of the assistant
governor approached that of a social work supervisor with specialized staff training responsibilities.

Meanwhile, in the study Administrative Consequences of Penal
Objectives, a conceptual framework is provided which makes it possible to pursue critically the idea of relating penal goals to staff
expertise and to the relationship of the so-called professional
and non-professional staffs. These have very significant staff-
training implications. For example, under a Passive Deterrence
regime the expertise of the non-professional, it is claimed, tends
to be concerned primarily with custodial matters and is in clear
contrast to the expertise of the professional whether they are in
the medical, social work or educational fields. The work of
professional and non-professional is seen as being highly compart-
mentalized. As one moves, however, from Passive Deterrence through
Active Deterrence and Passive Treatment to Active Treatment, the gap
between the expertise of the two narrows, and roles become defined

in terms of skills applied to common tasks, rather than in terms of
distinctive tasks. This may be seen as a not dissimilar situation
to that described by Bernstein in outlining the changes in the roles
and relationships of teachers of different subject specialisms, as a
school moves to the open model based on 'topic-centred interdisciplinary inquiry' rather than one where 'the subject is a clear-cut
definable unit in the curriculum'.

> We are moving from the secondary school where the teaching roles
> were insulated from each other, where the teacher had an
> organized area of authority and autonomy, to secondary schools
> where the teaching role is less autonomous and where it is a
> shared or co-operative role. There has been a shift from a
> teaching role which is, so to speak, 'given' (in the sense that
> one steps into assigned duties) to a role which has to be
> achieved in relation with other teachers. It is a role which is
> no longer made but has to be made. (10)

To return to the prison system, the shift from one penal goal to
another has implications not only for the relationship of professional and non-professional but also for the relationship between
one professional group and another, between the doctor, the psychologist, the minister of religion, the social worker and the education officer. The question may well be asked as to whether there
has been, or should be, a shift, in the case of professionals, from
roles which are 'given' to ones which are 'achieved', as one moves
from non-treatment to treatment institutions. Nor should the
question be confined to the treatment/training goals of prisons.
An equally provocative system of classification might be based on
security and/or control methods ranging from a basic dependency upon
psychological factors. This is implied by the Radzinowicz Committee
in its report 'The Regime for Long-Term Prisoners in Conditions of
Maximum Security' when they suggest that 'the medical officer and
psychologist have a special part to play in the work of explanation
of attitudes of prisoners and in helping staff to understand how to
cope with crises, even better, how to prevent them'. (11)

c Diversity v. uniformity - mobility and training

So far I have tried to emphasize that in examining an increasingly
large and diversified prison service it is helpful to use a variety
of different systems of classifying institutions in order to high-
light the problems of providing appropriate local structures and
relevant staffing and training resources. Equally important is the
need to identify the forces within the total prison organization
which appear to sustain diversity and those which seem to promote
uniformity. Two such forces are the system of promotion, linked
with mobility, and that of staff training. In the case of the
former, the pattern of mobility among governors is in marked contrast to that of the basic grade officer. Members of the governor
grade (12) are, throughout their whole career, unlikely to stay in
any one institution longer than four or five years. In a study of
assistant governors appointed between the mid-1950s and the later
1960s, it was shown that prior to first promotion two-thirds had
changed establishments at least once during their first five

years. (13)   Meanwhile, it is highly improbable that a governor who
has reached Governor II or Governor I rank, and who has almost
certainly changed institutions with each promotion, will have specialized in any one kind of institution. This system of mobility,
it is contended, will be an important source of change within a
particular institution but, because it militates against long-term
specialization and encourages the identification of a governor with
the service rather than with a particular establishment, it will be
an important force in promoting a more uniform approach throughout
the service as a whole. The position of the prison officers who are
not promoted to principal officer, on the other hand, is a force in
the opposite direction and indeed most prison officers are unlikely
to be promoted to principal officer until they have served at least
ten years. Unless they become specialists - for example, a hospital
officer - the chances are that they will stay at one establishment
for a considerable length of time, indeed some for the whole of
their career. (14)   One of the implications of this immobility,
which will be developed more fully later, is that a type of specialism among the discipline officers has developed which is both
the product of, and a reinforcement of, the process of diversification among penal institutions, and also a force towards maintaining
the status quo in the institution itself.

The second factor affecting the diversity-uniformity situation
other than mobility and promotion is the whole process of staff
training. Prison Service Staff Training may be divided into three
main areas: (a) the training provided centrally within the service,
principally at the Staff College and the two Officer Training
Schools, all of which come under the Principal of the Staff College;
(b) that organized within the different penal establishments or more
recently, regionally; and (c) that provided by outside educational
institutions such as universities, polytechnics and colleges of
further education. Perhaps the first point to observe is that the
prison service, like the police, but unlike the probation service,
relies much more on its own resources to provide the initial training. Whilst the probation service 'exports' its students to
universities and polytechnics for their initial one-year and two-
year courses and informally 'exports' its experienced professionals
to be tutors on such courses, the prison service 'imports' its
students and formally 'imports' university staff to assist in lec-
turing and advising at the Staff College and Officer Training
Schools. As a result, the prison service training system would seem
to encourage a more centralized and uniform approach as compared
with the probation service. This should be set against the possibility, however, that in terms of attitudes towards crime and punishment, probation attracts a more homogeneous and the prison service
a more heterogeneous group of recruits. Certainly a small survey
comparing groups of newly-joined assistant governors and newly-
joined probation officers indicated that this might well be the
case. (15)

The second point is the relative contribution to initial and subsequent training of prison personnel by the Staff College and the
Officer Training Schools on the one hand and by the different penal
establishments on the other. It is suggested that the greater the
emphasis on central training the greater the chances of uniformity,

whereas the more the emphasis in training is on local establishments the more opportunity there is for diversification. This is diffi- cult to quantify, but in terms of organized formal training the impression remains of the dominance of the Staff College and Officer Training Schools. In the case of the prison officer all recruits at present receive an initial training lasting three months, the first being spent in a penal establishment, very often a local prison, and the second and third at one of the OTSs. The officers may subse- quently return to the OTS for a two-week development course at the end of their probationary year. In the case of the assistant governor, of whom on average a third, in the 1960s, came from the prison officer class and two-thirds were newly-joined personnel, the initial training, up till 1973, had been an eight-month course organized by and held mainly in, the Staff College, with the assistant governor returning for one or two short courses during his two-year probationary period. Subsequent training at the Staff College, whilst originally planned to affect all members of the service, has tended to concentrate on those members of the prison officer and governor grades who were scheduled to be or had actually been, promoted, and those who were assuming specialist positions within the service. To this extent the central training organiza- tion appears to dominate the training scene. Its influence, fur- thermore, upon a general rather than a diversified approach to prison work is possibly increased by the marked tendency for course membership to be recruited on a general status basis rather than upon the basis of types of establishments, a system which also re- flects and emphasizes the prevailing hierarchical structure of the service. On the other hand, there has been a significant shift in recent years towards a more decentralized and diversified training programme. In the case of the prison officers, their initial train- ing is being seen increasingly as encompassed by a probationary training year, in which training in penal establishments is placed on a more systemic footing. In the case of the assistant governors, the eight-month course has been recently reorganized into a two- year 'sandwich' course, in which, ideally, the contribution at the Staff College is matched by an equally organized programme in establishments. At the same time, the curriculum-planning of the Staff College section is now based on the modular principle, and on an analysis of assistant governor roles in different establishments. This provides opportunities for work situations and problems in different type of institutions to be examined on the course from both a practical and a theoretical standpoint and thus supports the process of diversification. Meanwhile, at a post-experience level, the process of decentralization of training has developed in three main ways. First, many penal establishments have appointed staff training committees, which, together with full-time or part-time training officers, see their role as concerned with the development of continued training as well as of initial or induction training. Second, the regions have been developing a positive training role, in response to such significant innovations as observation and classification units, maximum security wings, and dispersal prisons, and to the new problems of security and control which have been experienced. Third, there is the relatively well-established prac- tice of providing some opportunity for individuals in the prison

service to attend full-time or day-release or part-time courses at
institutes of higher and further education.

2   PENAL AIMS AND METHODS - STAFFING AND TRAINING IN RELATION TO
    SPECIALISM

a   Changing aims and methods

It has already been emphasized that organization, staffing and
training should be examined in relation to the aims and functions of
different establishments of the prison service and to the range of
methods employed to achieve these aims. Reference might now be made
to a somewhat different but related point, namely that the organization, staffing and training of the prison service as a whole should
be related to changing priorities in aims and methods. In 'People
in Prison', it was emphasized that
    few large organizations have only one aim and it often obscures
    the real situation to try to bring all the activities of any one
    of them into one simple formula or slogan. Some of the confusion
    about the aims of the prison service arises from attempts to do
    so. (16)
Certainly prisons would appear in the first place to have the function, if not the aim, of punishment; then, the aim of containment
or security, whether this be in respect of the prisoner on trial
and/or awaiting sentence, or the sentenced prisoner; and finally,
the aim of rehabilitation, including, in the case of some prisoners
awaiting trial and sentence, a specifically diagnostic objective.
These aims may, in turn, be seen within the context of two main
constraints - those of humanity and control. The relative importance given to these aims, functions and constraints will vary not
only from institution to institution, but also from one period to
another. It would seem, in retrospect, that over the past decade
there have been three distinct periods. The mid-1960s reflected the
emphasis given to rehabilitation in the ACTO Report on After-Care
(1963), the late 1960s the importance attributed to security in the
Mountbatten Report (1966) and the early 1970s, the concern in the
Radzinowicz Report (1968) and 'People in Prison' (1969) with humane
containment. Over the same period, there was the succession of
challenge and counter-challenge to the methods of achieving these
aims. For example, both Mountbatten and Radzinowicz were concerned
with the problems of whether concentration or dispersal was the most
appropriate means of containing, in a humane manner, high security
risk prisoners. Inevitably, therefore, they raised questions about
the diagnosis of absconding and offending risks as a means of
selecting prisoners for maximum or minimum security conditions and
about the psychological as well as the physical means of containment.
The ACTO Report, in its turn, was part of the challenge to the
traditional rehabilitative methods of the earlier prison system,
which was based more on training through work, education and living
within a 'house' or 'wing' than on individual diagnosis, treatment
and the use of different techniques such as case-work, group-work
or community activity.   More specifically, it was pre-occupied with
the problems of after-care and with the use of appropriate skills

and structure for the effective return of offenders to society.
'People in Prison', meanwhile, may be seen as reflecting the reaction to the over-optimism of the rehabilitative approach, and as
an official introduction to the 'humane containment' ideology, with
an emphasis upon the more limited treatment objective of trying to
minimize the adverse effects of imprisonment. Finally, the 1967
Criminal Justice Act, with its introduction of parole may, in turn,
be interpreted as reinforcing the humane containment objective, in
that it sought to limit the ill-effects of imprisonment and at the
same time facilitate control and containment through the prospect
and reality of early release - a method, however, dependent upon
effectively predicting the risks of serious recidivism.

As different aims and methods were emphasized the problems of
effective staffing and training were raised and in particular the
question of the most appropriate source from which to secure relevant specialist skills - whether from within the service or from
without. It will not be possible within the confines of this short
section to examine comprehensively this basic question. Some of the
crucial issues, however, may be raised by looking at the status and
role of prison officers who, after all, constitute the dominant part
of the prison service.

b The prison officer - a specialist?

Prison officers indeed represent some three-quarters of the total
prison service staff. The most recent figures are given in
Table 2.2. (17)

TABLE 2.2

Date	Prison officers	Governors	Other non-industrial staff	Industrial staff	Total
1973 (1 Jan.)	13,172	505	3,205	1,987	18,869

The prison officer is recruited as a general prison officer rather
than a specialist, although the applicant and/or the selectors may
see him or her as a potential specialist. Specialism, however, may
emerge in one of three ways. First, he may be selected in the
relatively early stages of his career for a permanent or semi-
permanent specialist role. At the time of the White Paper on
'People in Prison' (1969), 7,500 of the 10,000 prison officers
carry out the general work of the establishment including, at a
local prison, the work at the courts. The remaining 2,500 have
chosen to specialise, at least for part of their career. The
specialists in this sense, include the instructors...the hospital officer, catering officer, physical education instructor,
the dog handlers and the trade assistants and works officers.
(18)
It may be noted that whilst most of these specialist roles are of

long standing, the dog handler is one example of a 'permanent' specialist role which has emerged in the past decade, in the wake of the Mountbatten Report. It may also be important to bear in mind that whilst all officers may be called upon to act in emergencies under the direction of the senior ranks of the general officer grade, most specialist officers are part of a distinct hierarchy. For example, the hospital officer is responsible through the hospital principal officer and the hospital chief to the prison medical officer. Given these distinct hierarchies, it is not surprising that side by side with the advantages of specialisms go the tensions between these specialists and the general discipline prison officer.

Second, specialism may emerge on a less permanent basis, being undertaken for perhaps three or four years at a spell. Some such specialisms are of long standing and are regarded as 'fixed posts' carrying with them considerable informal status and power, as, for example, the officer in charge of reception or 'the gate', or the court dock party. In this category may now be included relatively new specialist posts which reflect the changing emphasis on aims and methods. One example is the officer in the assessment and classifying teams which have developed to meet the new needs of both security and parole, and another is the senior officer who may be designated security officer.

Third, specialization may develop, almost without official recognition, as a result of the relative immobility of the general prison officer, once he has been posted to an establishment. A survey of officers passing through the OTS and Staff College during different periods in the 1960s on initial, development, or refresher training, confirmed the essentially different experiences of officers working in different types of establishments. One question which was asked referred to the jobs which afforded officers in different establishments the greatest job satisfaction. Some of the responses, which were clearly affected by job opportunity, were as in Table 2.3. (19)

TABLE 2.3   Job with most satisfaction

	2 years' experience			6 years + experience	
Locals		Borstals		Locals		Borstals
1 Courts	(105)	House board	(52)	Courts	(64)	Senior house officer	(40)
2 Reception	(99)	Landing/ House officer	(41)	Reception	(53)	Org. sport	(36)
3 Escort	(81)	Work party	(38)	Escort	(40)	House board	(36)
4 Gate	(77)	Org. sport	(37)	Gate	(36)	Landing/ house officer	(34)
5 Landing/ House officer	(71)	Group work	(28)	C.O.clerk	(25)	Group work	(29)
N*	212		88		121		96

* N is the total number of respondents under each heading.   The figures in parenthesis are responses.

These results can be interpreted in a variety of different ways. The high satisfaction, among prison officers in local prisons, from court and escort duties may be associated with monetary rewards or/and with the opportunity for getting out of the prison.   One interpretation, however, may be that in local prisons job satisfaction in court, reception, escort and to some extent gate duties is associated with a relationship between officer and prisoner, involving a large number of different people for limited periods of time but on what could be traumatic occasions for prisoners - sentencing, reception into prison, transfer to another prison.   This is contrasted with the group of borstal officers, where job satisfaction may be associated with a relationship involving a limited number of people, for a relatively long period of time, but in a variety of different contexts - a relationship which could be of prolonged significance.   The results, however, do tend to confirm the emergence of informal specialisms and raise the kind of questions about staff training posed earlier.   In this connection it is perhaps relevant to note the results of a study in which a sample of officers, who had been in the prison service some two years, were asked their opinions about initial training.   A significantly larger number of officers in local prisons (85 per cent) found the initial training helpful as compared with officers in other prisons (58 per cent) and youth establishments (62 per cent).   This tends to confirm that at the time of the study, the late 1960s, the initial training of officers was still dominated by the notion of the general prison officer, which probably meant the local prison officer, and this, despite the diversification of establishments and the growth of specialist duties.

The problem of specialism is not, of course, confined to within the prison officer ranks, but extends to the competition from the specialists who are imported from outside to the officers' attitudes to such competition, and to their expectations regarding their own future role.   What are the expectations of the prison officer? These start with the potential officer and obviously affect the whole recruitment and selection process.   On average some 10,000 people apply annually to become prison officers and just over one in ten, or between 1,000 and 1,500, are eventually appointed.   The process of selection therefore is not an inconsiderable one, involving written tests, medical examinations, interviews by one of four specially appointed interviewing teams, and the scrutiny which continues throughout the initial training and probationary year. Vocational motives are always difficult to determine, but evidence, based on the direct questioning of prison officers and by an analysis of recruitment trends in relationship to the economic state of the country, both emphasize the importance attached to the security which the job affords.   Nevertheless, there is ample evidence that there are other strong motives.   The newly-recruited officer is, on average, in his late 20s with either a number of years experience as a skilled worker (a clear majority belonged to this class) or in about a third of the cases, regular military experience.   A positive desire for job change appears, therefore, to be evident in the majority of cases.   Meanwhile, in terms of intelligence, he is in

the top third of the population, but educationally a disproportionately low number have had grammar school education or its equivalent
or have left school at 16 or over, although the situation was changing towards the end of the 1960s. There is some suggestion, therefore, of the prison officer being a person with a sense of under-
achievement, seeking a more personally rewarding vocation. Indeed,
a sample of newly-appointed officers questioned in 1971 regarded
their appointment to the prison service as a distinct rise in status.
Asked to rate their old job and their new one against a list of
thirty occupations, the new job, that of prison officer, was on
average more than six places higher in the status rating. The precise nature of their aspirations and expectations about their prison
role may well, of course, vary from time to time depending partly
upon the prevailing penal climate. Certainly in the mid-1960s,
post-ACTO but pre-Mountbatten, expectations about the future role
tended to be towards that of the social worker. Given several
occupations (police, foreman, nurse, probation officer, youth leader,
teacher, NCO) to compare with their future role as prison officer,
the most frequent response, irrespective of the type of establishments at which they were serving, was the probation officer. Such
aspirations or expectations, whether directed towards the status, or
the role, or both, of the social worker encountered, however, three
problems. The first was that, assuming social work requires a
distinctive set of attitudes about such matters as responsibility,
punishment, and treatment, the majority of prison officers do not
appear to share these. Asked to respond to a series of questions on
crime and punishment which statistically distinguished between the
attitudes of social workers and magistrates along a 'rehabilitation
- retribution/deterrence' continuum, the newly-appointed prison
officers, whilst showing a wide distribution of attitudes, out-
deterred the magistrates. Interestingly, groups of newly-appointed
assistant governors had, however, an average score identical with
that of the newly-appointed probation officers, which in itself
raises questions about the professional relationship of assistant
governors with prison officers and probation officers within the
prison system. The second problem facing the specialist social work
aspirations of the prison officer is his sense of professional or
vocational security. The prison officer, far more than the assistant governor or the probation officer, appears to experience a
conflict in that whilst he regards his position as a worthy one, he
thinks that the general public does not share this belief. In a
study previously mentioned, newly-appointed probation officers,
assistant governors and prison officers were asked to rate, in
order of status, thirty occupations and then to indicate where on
the list they would place their own job. They were also asked to
show where they believed the general public would place their
occupations. Whilst there was a close relationship between 'self'
and 'public' rating by probation officers and assistant governors,
particularly the former, there was a wide gap in the rating by
prison officers, as shown in Table 2.4.

TABLE 2.4

	Rating of own occupation	Estimate of public opinion rating	Difference
Probation officer	6.5	7.5	+ 1
Assistant governor	3.0	6.0	+ 3
Prison officer	9.5	16.5	+ 7

If prison officers do take this perception and this conflict into the prison service, then it may have serious implications for their ability to act in a social work capacity with prisoners, who can so easily present them with additional status problems. It has been maintained, and with some supportive evidence, for example, that one way in which prisoners cope with the deprivation of imprisonment and the consequential threats to self-esteem is by lowering the status of the prison officer and thereby, relatively, raising their own.

And finally, the third problem to specialist aspirations of the prison officer is the increasing number of outside specialists introduced into the prison service, whether these be the psychologists, education officers, or probation officers assuming a prison welfare officer role. This is, of course, not to imply that these outside specialists have not had their own problems. The psychologists, for example, were introduced into the prison service following the 1948 Criminal Justice Act, primarily in order to prepare reports to court, but their subsequent experience was one of role change and adaptations and a search for a prison identity, which now includes a strong element of staff training and research. The probation officer-cum-welfare officer, meanwhile, had to come to terms with dual accountability since, being seconded for, probably, only a limited period of time, he has professional responsibility to his superior in the probation service and work responsibility to the prison governor. This dual accountability indeed raises questions of fundamental importance about the character of secondment and its importance in determining the nature and kind of influence which the outside specialist can bring to bear within and without the penal establishment. It is perhaps his position as a seconded person, as much as his professional status and skills, that makes his relationship with the prison officer at one and the same time problematic but potentially productive. Donald Schon, in his Reith lectures on Dynamic Conservatism, (20) emphasized that one source of change in an institution was through invasion. An important function of the specialist invaders of prisons may therefore be that, coming from a different vocational and professional culture, they challenge the basic assumptions and values of the prevailing prison system. The implications of this invasion are heightened in that specialists have the life-line of secondment, which provides some protection from their 'humane containment' by the prisons. The interreaction of the prison staff and specialist invaders may be productive in that both the forces of conservatism and those of change are essential ingredients of a healthy organization. It may be problematic in that relative independence is seen as a source of irresponsibility.

The prison officer has been used as one example within a prison service in which changing and diverse aims and methods have created problems of specialist resources. The position of the assistant governor is equally problematical and challenging, partly because recruitment from within the service and from without raises questions about the sources of change and stability within the service; partly because, starting as a specialist housemaster within the borstal system, the position of assistant governor has relatively recently expanded into the prisons and is now less a role than a status; and also partly because the influx of specialists has, as with the officer, raised basic issues about the distinctive contribution which the assistant governors and, indeed, the governor, do and should make in institutions having distinctive objectives and methods.

It is, perhaps, pertinent to conclude this section by asking whether the aim of 'human containment' which appears to be the official aim of the prison service in the 1970s enables the relative contribution of the prison officer, the assistant governor and governor, and the specialists to be more clearly and realistically defined. It seems in one sense to be a historical compromise which retains the primacy of security, but within the constraints of a humane approach. This approach, in turn, emphasizes the importance of the quality of life in the present, particularly for long-term prisoners, and also the more realistic objective of reducing the adverse effects of imprisonment on the future conduct of released prisoners. It reflects the reaction to criticism of prison service's containment skills as embodied in the Mountbatten Report; to the uncertainty about a positive and experimental rehabilitation role in face of the criminological researcher's inability to establish significant relative success rates; and to the concern engendered by the studies of total institutions and the effects of deprivation in such institutions. But does it also reflect a conscious or unconscious attempt to provide an aim which retains the notion of one prison service in the face of increasing size and diversification; to provide a generic element to the professional skills of governors whose promotion structure has traditionally required mobility and non-specialization; to reduce, in appearance or reality, the conflict and insecurity within the general prison officer role; and to 'contain' within the embrace of humanity the experimental role of the specialist from outside?

NOTES

1 Home Office, 'People in Prison: England and Wales', London, 1969, p. 88.
2 Ibid., p. 13.
3 Eleventh Report from the Estimates Committee, Session 1966-7, 'Prisons, Borstals and Detention Centres', para. 10.
4 'People in Prison', p. 100.
5 Home Office, 'Report on the Work of the Prison Department', London, 1972, p. 9, pp. 86-7.
6 Ibid., Appendix 3. Also 'People in Prison', p. 89.

7   N. A. Jepson, Learning and Experience, 'Prison Service Journal',
    no. 10, April 1973. See also N. A. Jepson, The Value of Prison,
    'Howard Journal of Penology', vol. XIII, no. 3, 1972.
8   G. Rose, Administrative Consequences of Penal Objectives in
    P. Halmos (ed.), 'Sociological Studies in the British Penal
    Service', Keele, 1965, pp. 211-36.
9   A. E. Bottoms and F. H. McClintock, 'Criminals Coming of Age',
    Heinemann, London, 1973.
10 B. Bernstein, Open Schools, Open Society, 'New Society', 14 Sep-
    tember 1967.
11 Report of the Advisory Council on the Penal System, 'The Regime
    for Long-Term Prisoners in Conditions of Maximum Security', 1968.
12 The ranks of the prison office grade are: prison officer;
    senior officer; principal officer; chief officer II; chief
    officer I. The ranks of the governor grade are: assistant
    governor II; assistant governor I; governor III; governor II;
    governor I.
13 N. A. Jepson, 'The Recruitment and Training of Assistant
    Governors: Evidence submitted to Home Office Working Party on
    Prison Officers', London, 1970.
14 A survey of over a thousand officers during the 1960s indicated
    that a discipline officer, once posted from the Officer Training
    School, would be most likely to stay at that one institution for
    at least six years. Ninety per cent of the sample had served in
    only one establishment after two years, and nearly two-thirds
    after six years. The amount of detached duty (i.e. temporary
    duty in another establishment) was at that time limited - less
    than one in five had been on detached duty in the first two
    years and half were without the experience after six years.
    Detached duty may well have increased, however, during the
    1970s.
15 See Table 2.4. Whilst the mean scores of the two groups were
    the same the standard deviations were significantly different.
16 'People in Prison', p. 7.
17 'Report on the Work of the Prison Department', p. 9.
18 'People in Prison', p. 93.
19 These and subsequent statistics are taken from surveys carried
    out by N. Jepson at the Prison Service Staff College and OTSs
    during the period 1964-71.
20 D. Schon, Dynamic Conservatism, 'Listener', 26 November 1970.

Chapter 3

ASPECTS OF THE PSYCHOLOGY OF IMPRISONMENT

Mark Williams

Existing penal arrangements are neither easily described nor readily simplified. Equally, the work of the prison psychologist is varied, and necessarily sometimes idiosyncratic. What follows, therefore, is essentially a personal interpretation of just part of what has been done by psychologists working in prison. Obviously, it does not represent the views of the Home Office, and any impressions, misleading or otherwise, are the responsibility of the author alone.

The central problem of imprisonment is surely this: that institutions designed for custody must be organized in such a way as to influence behaviour following release. This task is equivalent to the provision of institutional rules to govern personal conduct, but with the crucial difference that the rules are to be applied in one context, and yet their effect must be apparent in another. The official view is set out in 'People in Prison' (Home Office, 1969):

> The 'humane containment' of offenders cannot be the sole task of the Prison Service. If, as the late Sir Alexander Paterson put it, prison is seen only as a cloakroom in which the enemy of society is duly deposited till called for after a fixed period, the protection afforded to society is temporary and the offender may return to the community more embittered and anti-social than before. It has been the aim of the Service, since the turn of the century, to attempt the more constructive and more difficult task of releasing offenders who, in the well-known words of the Gladstone Committee, might be 'better men and women, physically and morally, than when they came in'. A variety of terms, reflecting the complexity and uncertainty of the task, have been used to describe this attempt: reformation, re-education, treatment, training, rehabilitation.

The very diversity of this list of descriptions is surely indicative of the fact that there is at present no proven recipe for success. But this is hardly surprising. The great majority of crime is voluntary and purposive behaviour (and this is reflected at every level; for example, over 60 per cent of the adult males in prison have simply been sentenced for acts of dishonesty). In many ways it resembles other 'bad habits' - smoking, alcoholism, drug addiction, overeating, gambling - that seem if anything to have increased with contemporary affluence, and yet at the same time to have remained

peculiarly resistant to social control. The existence of the victim
creates pressure for more forceful intervention against crime, but
this in itself entails no greater prospect of success.

The official view is quite explicit in its warnings against over-
optimistic claims for 'treatment', without in any way denying its
importance as a task.

> No clear distinction can, or should, be drawn between the aspects
> of treatment that are primarily designed to regulate the daily
> life of an offender in custody and those that look primarily
> towards his return to the community...it is wrong to think of
> treatment as an item, or choice of items, that can be added at
> will to the daily regime of a prison or borstal to meet the needs
> of offenders. Neither our capacity for the diagnosis of the
> needs of offenders nor the ability to effect a cure is at present
> as great as many advocates of this or that form of treatment have
> implied. We need a view of treatment that embraces all that is
> done by or for the offender in custody. But there is also a
> place in the prison system for the use of the term in the alter-
> native sense in which it relates to a diagnosis and to the possi-
> bility of a changed way of life; and there are already in the
> system a wide variety of forms of treatment that have been
> evolved in the hope that they may directly affect an offender's
> behaviour both in custody and after release....('People in
> Prison').

For the remainder of this discussion, therefore, the custodial
function of prisons will be taken as axiomatic, and more detailed
analysis reserved for attempts at treatment (in the widest sense of
the word) aimed at post-institutional behaviour-change.

The work of the prison psychologist is summarized in 'People in
Prison' as follows:

> When psychologists were first appointed to the Prison Service,
> their role was seen mainly as the assessment of prisoners on
> remand, and some psychologists still do this work in local
> prisons or remand centres. Others work in allocation centres
> contributing to the initial assessment of prisoners received on
> conviction, and others in training prisons where the task may be
> that of assessing change in attitudes and behaviour during
> sentence. Whatever the area of his work, the psychologist aims
> to provide recommendations on which operational decisions may be
> made and to collect data for evaluative research into the effec-
> tiveness of the system to which he is contributing. Psycholo-
> gists have played a considerable part in the development of group
> counselling...and they take training and support groups for the
> staff engaged on this work. In his general approach to his work
> in the Prison Service, the psychologist aims to assess and under-
> stand institutional processes and the ways in which they can
> affect both prisoner and staff.

Obviously, the initial emphasis on individual assessments is in line
with the remarks cited earlier on the requirement for the 'diagnosis'
of the 'needs' of the offender and his 'suitability' for the
'variety of forms' of treatment already in existence. The apparent
shift to more general areas of concern, therefore, is indicative of
the significant constraints on assessment in prison; constraints
that are important and deserving of further consideration.

Once an offender has been given a custodial sentence, the
question of his assessment is inextricably bound up with that of his
'treatment'. The basic rationale is that different people require
different treatments; that what might be good for one need not be
so for another, and, indeed, could be positively harmful. Accordingly, therefore, any attempt to increase the efficacy of 'treatment'
is critically dependent on the ability to identify those for whom
the 'treatment' is 'suitable'. And in this context, a suitable case
for treatment is one whose likelihood of reconviction is significantly reduced by the application of that treatment. Granted such a
model, few would deny the claims of the psychologist to assist in
its operation. But in practice the results have been, to say the
least, ambiguous.

It is certainly true that psychologists have been able to predict
the post-release behaviour of offenders. A good example occurs in
the series of investigations of corrective trainees (that is, those
sentenced to Corrective Training; a sentence that has since been
dropped, but which was intended originally as an adult equivalent to
Borstal Training) reported by Taylor (1960, 1964). For one group,
the accuracy of psychological prognosis was reasonably good (see
Table 3.1).

TABLE 3.1

	Prognosis: chances of future reconviction		
	Better than Evens	Evens	Less than Evens
No. not reconvicted	58	73	17
No. reconvicted	27	72	47

But drawbacks are apparent. First, the largest proportion are
placed in the 'Average' column, which clearly has the least practical utility. More important, however, is the fact the prognosis as
such confounds the specifically psychological aspects of the judgment with the information already known to predict reconviction
(such as the number of previous convictions, age at onset of criminal activity, etc.). It has proved extremely difficult to find
items, other than aspects of criminal history, that are related to
reconviction. In the same report, for example, the inmate's initial
attitude to his sentence (responsive, apathetic or hostile) was not
a significant predictor of post-release behaviour, whereas the
number of previous convictions, and the presence or otherwise of an
intact marriage, were. Nor must it be assumed that psychological
prognosis is invariably successful. Taylor reported the result of
prognosis made shortly prior to discharge (see Table 3.2).

TABLE 3.2

	Prognosis: Chance of future reconviction		
	Better than Evens	Evens	Less than Evens
No. not reconvicted	12	21	30
No. reconvicted	10	16	29

A very similar result was obtained from the governors of the dis-
charging institution, so the apparent uncertainty was not restricted
to psychologists. A possible inference from these data is that when
an inmate is assessed on entry into the system, then the prognosis
is reasonably accurate because of the weight given to the objective
features of his history. As the inmate passes through the system,
however, greater weight is given to his institutional performance,
and this unfortunately is an invalid basis for judgment. Taylor
himself summed up the results as follows:

> There was evidence that it was possible to discriminate between
> the more responsive and the less responsive men at training
> prisons...yet subsequent events have shown that...none of these
> factors in themselves were associated with reconviction. Fur-
> ther, men who were declared to be less responsive to training did
> neither better nor worse on release than men who had been con-
> sidered to be responsive. In fact, behaviour in prison of
> corrective trainees does not appear to be directly related to
> behaviour out of prison.

More significantly,

> Those factors which did emerge as being related to reconviction/
> non-reconviction were not of a kind which might indicate which
> type of trainee is most likely to benefit from training.

In so far as the work of the prison psychologist consisted of the
assessment of suitability for treatment, this laconic conclusion had
obvious implications!

A more elaborate piece of research gives added substance to this
result. Between October 1958 and June 1959, information was collected about 438 adults serving their first sentence of imprisonment
and 242 adults who had served one previous sentence of either
imprisonment or borstal training. The latter were referred to as
'primary recidivists' for the simple reason that, in contrast to
those serving their first sentence, the majority would return to
prison for at least one further spell. The two samples were therefore designated by the initials FS (first sentence) and PR (primary
recidivist). The follow-up of the greater part of the total sample
allowed a further contrast, since members of both groups were
ultimately reconvicted or not reconvicted. The results of this
follow-up (reported in 'Some Correlates of Primary Recidivism',
1966) certainly substantiated the original distinction, with reconviction rates of approximately one in three for the FS sample, and
two in three for that of the PRs:

TABLE 3.3

	F S	P R
Not reconvicted	251	77
Reconvicted	154	158

In the comparison between the FS and PR samples, 40 significant differences were found, representing almost half of the attributes considered. Fewer of these attributes were considered in the follow-up, but one important feature emerged. Of 19 particular differences between the FS and PR samples, 13 were also present between FSs who were reconvicted (the next generation of PRs) and those who were not. But the number of differences had dropped to only three when comparison was made between the reconvicted and non-reconvicted PRs. This possibly confusing picture may be summarized very simply: the major difference between individuals in prison is between those serving their first sentence and the rest. Table 3.3 is a part of this: no single attribute more strongly differentiated the first sentence and the primary recidivist groups than the subsequent history of offending. And since those on first sentence constitute a minority of the prison population, the classic task of assessment for treatment has to deal with an increasingly homogeneous population (homogeneous, that is, in respect of the kinds of attribute predictive of penal failure).

Greater success in this kind of area is described by Shapland (1969b). Of course, the detention centre is an institution designed for the young offender, and hence of particular interest. In discussion with detention centre staff and After-Care Officers, there was general agreement that the more a boy departed from the 'normal' the less likely he was to benefit from the detention centre regime. A sample of 400 boys was therefore interviewed by psychologists and amongst the data collected was the following:

My impression at the end of the interview as to whether the boy had 'odd features' or not. Odd features in this sense is difficult to describe. The judgment was based on information available in the boy's record and information verbal and non-verbal from the interview.

One-third of the sample was rated as 'odd', but psychological test data were not used in this essentially subjective judgment (being available only after the judgment). This is perhaps the classic picture of the psychologist working his interpretative magic in an interview situation (and is given added substance by the demonstration in the pilot study that detention staff rated only 7 per cent as 'odd', compared with the psychologist's 43 per cent; Shapland, 1969a). But the outcome was encouraging: the psychologist's rating of 'odd' was the best single predictor of reconviction (and this rating was, of course, unknown to those actually dealing with the boys). A lot of statistical material was also presented, but this in itself was a simple yet effective demonstration that a valid assessment of suitability for the detention centre sentence remains a possibility.

Not so encouraging was the result of a more elaborate experiment involving borstal trainees. During 1965 and 1966 over 600 of these were allocated at random to one of three comparable institutions, each of which exemplified a different approach to treatment (Williams, 1970). Prior to his allocation, the trainee was assessed, and included in that assessment was a global prediction of post-institutional outcome, and a specific prediction of the outcome for each of the three possible institutions. Thus, every trainee had a general prediction, and a specific prediction for the institution to which he was in fact ultimately allocated. In the follow-up subsequent to discharge, both of these predictions could be verified. The results of the general prediction were as in Table 3.4.

TABLE 3.4

	Probable success	Possible success	Possible failure	Probable failure
No. in category	35	230	269	69
% reconvicted	48.6	58.3	65.4	75.4

Obviously, the four groups are clearly distinguishable, although again the greatest numbers fall in the intermediate categories. However, when the prediction was made for the individual at his actual destination, the results were quite different (see Table 3.5).

TABLE 3.5

	Probable success	Possible success	Possible failure	Probable failure
No. in category	81	210	214	94
% reconvicted	63	57.1	65.9	68.1

In this case, the extreme categories were more readily utilized, but the differentiation no longer had a consistent relationship with outcome. The results taken together seem to suggest that the marginal ability psychological staff have to predict the outcome of borstal training may disappear given knowledge of the specific treatment actually applied. Furthermore, this has an obvious similarity to the results cited earlier concerning corrective trainees; both are demonstrations of the apparent misleading influence of 'inside' knowledge.

More objective approaches to psychological assessment of the offender centre on the psychological test. The results of a great deal of academic and professional work over the past decades have produced little systematic knowledge, however. One of the few consistent findings has been that incarcerated offenders are more 'neurotic' than the norm, particularly when the measure of neuroticism has been from the Eysenck Personality Inventory (an example is Fitch, 1961). Even this relationship has recently been called into question, however. Hardwick (1974) presented the Eysenck Inventory to groups of prisoners, some of whom were instructed to respond 'as you usually feel when you're not in prison' and others 'as you feel now, in prison.' The results of this simple expedient were such as to suggest two things: first, that the supposed neuroticism of the imprisoned is transitory rather than fundamental, and the second, that it is a result rather than a cause of imprisonment. A not un- expected finding (in hindsight), and one reminiscent of the suggestion of Cohen and Taylor that drug-takers might not be para- noid, as is suggested by some test results, but instead that they are in reality persecuted!

Enough research has been described to suggest the serious limita- tions to what might be termed traditional psychological applications in routine prison work. A separate and distinct area of research has been to the effectiveness not of psychologists, but of the treatment which offenders have been offered. The experiment involv- ing a random allocation of borstal trainees to three institutions provided a rigorous basis for estimating the comparative success of three possible approaches, designated 'traditional', 'casework' and 'group counselling' (see Fisher, 1967, for descriptions of these regimes, and Williams, 1970, for details of the experimental design and outcome). The two-year follow-up is displayed in Figure 3.1 in the form of cumulative reconviction curves; showing at monthly intervals following release just what proportion have been convicted of a further offence.

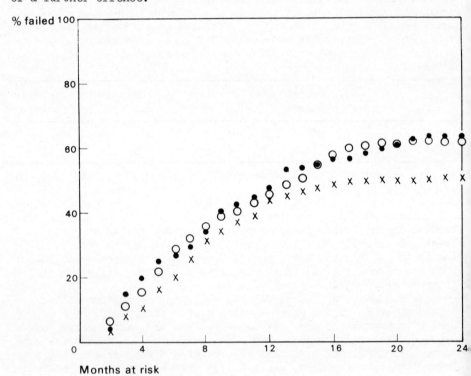

FIGURE 3.1

Some comments on this result are in order here. First, the slight
superiority of the casework institution is statistically significant
- it is unlikely to have occurred by chance alone. But the difference is small, and the overall failure rate is high (especially
since these are small open borstals that should have results amongst
the best in the borstal system). Furthermore, each institution
seemed to succeed with the same sorts of individual; in particular,
the casework regime did not do especially well with those cases
assessed in the allocation centre as requiring casework. Considerations such as these have tended to reduce the practical utility of
this result, and there has not been a proliferation of institutions
run on casework lines in the prison system.

Possibly the most notable development of recent years has been
the creation of a new prison at Grendon Underwood - an institution
specializing in the investigation and treatment of the so-called
psychopath (and often referred to as a psychiatric prison). Newton
(1969, 1971) presented the results of a series of comparisons of
various groups treated at Grendon with groups from other prisons.
One such comparison was between 87 Grendon inmates matched with 87
inmates of a neighbouring local prison, Oxford (and these inmates
were matched by year of release, approximate age on conviction,
number of previous convictions, length of sentence and type of
offence). The result of a four-year follow-up is displayed in
Figure 3.2, with a four-year reconviction total of about 65 per
cent.

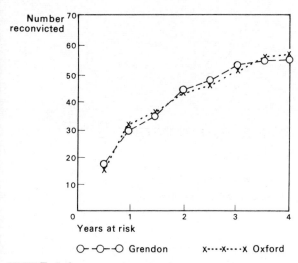

FIGURE 3.2

The reconviction rates correspond closely at all points, making
assertions of a Grendon treatment-effect difficult to sustain. The
other results are no less discouraging; as the author herself con-
cludes (Newton 1971):
> any change in selection policy would have to be on a strictly
> experimental basis, as none of the results so far lead to the
> conclusion that any particular type of patients does any better
> than the rest at Grendon...all we can conclude from research

results so far is that, for the men we receive, the treatment has
not been shown to be effective in the period after release.
Objections have been raised to this conclusion, however (see Scott,
(1973) and, of course, objections to the objections (Williams, 1973;
Hickey, 1974)!
    The efficacy of penal methods may be inferred from the effects of
changes in procedure that are not in themselves deliberate attempts
to improve treatment. Thus, in a borstal with extensive psychiatric
resources, there was a considerable reduction in the average time
served which was the result of an increase in the population rather
than any attempt to shorten or streamline the treatment process.
The effect of this change can be seen in a contrast between a 1965
and a 1968 sample of inmates. The result is displayed in Figure 3.3.

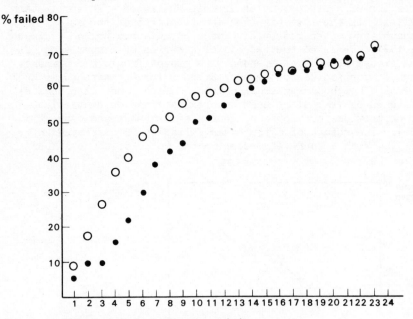

Time before conviction (months)

● 1965: Average time served 14·68 months
○ 1968: Average time served 11·24 months

FIGURE 3.3

The apparent difference in the early months of release could be due
to chance alone, and by eighteen months the results are virtually
identical. It is obviously questionable whether a treatment with a
two-year reconviction rate of 70 per cent can be considered effective, especially when a reduction of almost 25 per cent in treatment
duration makes no apparent difference to treatment outcome. On the
other hand, of course, such 'natural' experiments are inevitably
ambiguous, being open to more than one interpretation. Ultimately,
the effectiveness of otherwise of treatment procedures is dependent
on properly designed experiments, akin to the clinical trials of the
psychiatric and medical professions. Prison psychologists have

utilized existing data in the analysis of institutional processes, but a persistent demand has been for controlled experiments. A good example of this kind of organizational aspect may be found at the industrial prison at Coldingley. Here the Psychological Department have from very early on used sophisticated statistical techniques to monitor the effectiveness of the new institution, and the results of the first five years are now due. Whatever the outcome, the importance of this work is surely that the knowledge of results is comparatively quick and unambiguous.

The results of much of this research exert a continuing influence on the organization of the prison system, particularly in respect of the young offender. The emergence of the so-called Neighbourhood Borstal has been presented by a Prison Administrator (Faulkner, 1974) thus:

> The borstal system has traditionally included a sophisticated process of assessment intended to identify the needs and characteristics of the individual offender and to allocate him to a training establishment designed to match those needs and characteristics with an appropriate programme of training. Each establishment has thus been identified with a particular type of offender, and the number of establishments to which a particular individual might be sent has naturally been small ...the results of research give no grounds for thinking that specialised establishments of the traditional kind are particularly effective in influencing an offender's conduct...the 'Neighbourhood' or 'Community' institution attempts to break away from this tradition. Its essential features are that its population is drawn from a fairly compact and local area, and that most offenders from its area who receive the appropriate custodial sentence will go to that establishment. It thus has ...a more mixed population than the traditional training borstal.

More radical perhaps is the stress given to non-custodial measures for young offenders in the recent Report of the Advisory Council on the Penal System (Home Office, 1974) which is justified as follows:

> Sooner or later almost every offender sent to custody must rejoin society; and a way should be found of dealing with young adult offenders which does not defeat the object of protecting the public by eventually releasing from custody a more determined offender. Neither practical experience nor the results of research in recent years have established the superiority of custodial over non-custodial methods in their effect upon renewed offending: this is still an open question. Some aspects of custodial treatment may even contribute to recidivism. Moreover, comparisons of different types of custodial regime have so far shown little or no difference in effects upon offending again. This suggests that the treatment effort, whatever its nature, has very little impact compared with the general social experiences and pressures of living in a custodial establishment, and with the environmental influences and opportunities which the offender meets on release.

And finally, of course, is the effect of this research on the organization of the psychologists themselves.

An example of the kind of evolution possible in the organization of psychologists is the recent establishment of a group of prison psychologists with special responsibilities in providing for the young offender (the 17 to 21 year age group). Traditionally, a large proportion of the psychological resources have been allocated to the Young Offender system, but the predominant use of this resource was for individual assessment. Emphasis on the young offender has not changed. But in setting up a Young Offender Psychology Unit, explicit recognition is given to the necessity for the evaluation of daily practice (including change) as and when it occurs. Of course, such evaluation is by no means the limit of psychological involvement in the prison system. Sufficient is known of the effects of imprisonment to establish that the central problem surely remains; namely, what should actually be done to individuals in custody to reduce their probability of re-offending. But advice from psychologists should have the additional (and possibly unique feature that any suggestions for change should include within them the means whereby such change can be objectively evaluated.

REFERENCES

FAULKNER, D.E.R. (1974), The Neighbourhood Borstal, in 'The Southfield Papers', The Southfield Trust, London.
FISHER, R.M. (1967), 'The assessment of the effects of English Borstal boys of different correctional training and treatment programs', PhD(Soc) thesis, University of London.
FITCH, J.H. (1961), 'Two Personality Variables and their Distribution in a Criminal Population', Psychologists Monograph, no.11.
HARDWICK, A.E. (1974), 'The effect of "inside" and "outside" instructions on P.E.N.L. and H.D.H.Q. scores of Young Prisoners', unpublished.
HICKEY, P. (1974), Grendon: Further Comment, 'Prison Service Journal', no. 14 (new series).
HOME OFFICE (1969), 'People in Prison', HMSO, London.
HOME OFFICE (1974, 'Young Adult Offenders', HMSO, London.
NEWTON, M. (1969), 'Reconviction of Borstal Boys who received Treatment at H.M. Prison, Grendon', CP Report, no. 27.
NEWTON, M. (1971), 'Reconviction after treatment at Grendon', unpublished.
OFFICE OF THE CHIEF PSYCHOLOGIST (1966), 'Some Correlates of Primary Recidivism', Psychologists Monograph, no. 17.
SCOTT, P.D. (1973), Grendon Under Disputation, 'Prison Service Journal', no. 9 (new series).
SHAPLAND, P. (1969a), 'Detention Centre Research - a pilot study at Whatton Detention Centre', CP Report, no. 24.
SHAPLAND, P. (1969b), 'Factors associated with Success and Failure in Senior Detention Centres', Psychologists Monograph, no. 19.
TAYLOR, R.S. (1960, 1964), 'Follow-up Studies of Corrective Trainees', Part A, Part B, Part C. Psychologists Monograph, no. 6.
WILLIAMS, M. (1970), 'A Study of some aspects of Borstal Allocation', CP Report, no. 33.
WILLIAMS, M. (1973), Grendon Still Under Disputation, 'Prison Service Journal', no. 11 (new series).

Chapter 4

THE IMPRISONMENT OF FEMALES

Frances Heidensohn

For most of its history, the prison system of England and Wales has
not significantly differentiated between its male and female inmates; in more recent times, however, this approach has changed
somewhat. In this chapter I shall look briefly at the history of
women's imprisonment and in the light of growing emphasis on a
'special' approach to it, consider women's recorded criminality and
societal reaction to it and the particular problems involved in
putting women in prison.

Punitive imprisonment is of relatively recent origin. Prior to
its general introduction, fines, mutilation and capital punishment
were used, and imposed on women as on men, with only a few minor
modifications: thus, for example, women were burnt for some offences rather than hanged and publicly exhibited. They were also
allowed to 'plead their bellies' until their child was born. It was
because of their lower official criminality rather than judicial or
legislative leniency that far fewer women than men suffered these
fiscal and corporal penalties.

As Bridewells and the custodial use of gaols developed, women,
vagabonds, whores and thieves were thrust into them (literally) with
men. No distinction as to age or sex was made; the 1729 Commons
Committee on 'the state of Gaols in this kingdom' saw in the Mar-
shalsea prison 'both men and women lying, at the point of death, on
the bare filthy rags'. Howard and the prison reformers in the
eighteenth century thought that separation of the sexes was a sufficient reform and that women prisoners presented no other special
problems. But in 1813, Elizabeth Fry visited Newgate and saw 'three
hundred women...and...their multitudes of children' (Smith, 1962).
Fry began (in 1817) her Ladies' Association to help women prisoners.
Provision for women was included in the 'model' prisons built in
Britain from the 1840s on, and although now segregated, their regime
differed only in tiny details (e.g. a softer pillow and an iron bed
rather than a plank) from the men's. A three-stage system for women
convicts was planned by Jebb, using Millbank, Brixton and Fulham.
Later Parkhurst and a new prison at Woking were used.
Apart from the introduction of female wardresses, the prison

system for women remained based as closely as possible on the men's for at least a century. As Ruggles-Brise (1921) put it, 'the method of dealing with criminal women has (not) engaged that close attention which might have been expected from the nature and difficulty and importance of the problem. The law strikes men and women indifferently with the same penalties of penal servitude and imprisonment. In the case of women it only provides that they shall be separated from the other sex: that they shall be in the charge of female officers and...relieved from the harder forms of labour.' Ruggles-Brise was referring to his own period and Jebb's and Du Cane's before that.

In 1945 after half a century of steady decline in the annual female prison population (from about 50,000 in 1895 to 33,000 in 1913 and 11,000 in 1921) the Prison Commissioners reported that 'save for the sex and clothing of prisoners and staff it would not be easy for an unskilled observer to distinguish any difference between a men's prison and a women's prison' (Home Office, 1947). Some need to distinguish between men and women prisoners was now being felt, but at this stage it took the form of concentrating the diminishing female population in fewer and fewer establishments, and in more relaxations in regime details, e.g. on uniform, physical surroundings, etc. The developments of this century for women have paralleled those for men - an established borstal system, open prisons and even, for a briefer period, a girls' Detention Centre; for the 1877 Act, centralizing prison administration, had aimed, as Du Cane (1885) put it, to apply 'to all prisoners, wherever confined, ...a uniform system of punishment, devised to effect in the best method that which is the greater object of punishment, viz. the repression of crime; and economy in the expense of prisons'. Despite gallons of pastel paint on old prison walls, cretonne flowery curtains over windows, this uniformity, despite increased sex segregation, applied to the female prison regime till recently; today its effects largely remain.

In December 1968, James Callaghan, the then Home Secretary, announced plans to build a new Holloway prison for women and declared a change in emphasis and approach to female offenders in custody (Hansard, 16 December 1968). A new, purpose-built women's prison was, in itself, novel; mostly, women had been kept in institutions built for other purposes: the old Holloway is a mid-nineteenth-century house of correction, Styal is a former children's home. Remarkable too was the different and special approach to treating women, based on the notion that those few offending seriously and frequently enough to warrant imprisonment must be physically and/or mentally in need of therapy. Henceforward the female system was to be therapeutically oriented with the new Holloway as its centre. Yet historically, as I have indicated, women had neither been given special treatment nor been subjected to other than a modified male regime.

Were then women offenders once more similar to their male counterparts than today? Or have they always been different with special needs and problems with treatment changes only becoming possible as greater resources were made available and the special problems studied? We need to look at women offenders in general, their treatment and its effects, especially when in custody. Once

barely of academic interest, these topics have been increasingly and
significantly studied in more recent times.

I OFFENDING WOMEN

Quetelet long ago observed that women make a startingly small contribution to recorded criminality. Of course, police statistics and
court records are.only annual accounts which control agencies are
required to give of their activities; they reflect police (and
other) selections of encounters with and between the public and not
any total range of such events, which must remain unknowable.
Nevertheless, the outcomes of recorded encounters are real enough
and have important consequences for both those involved and for the
provision of care. In 1972 of 1,826,236 persons found guilty by
courts in England and Wales only 164,948, or 9 per cent, were females, a ratio of 10:1 which has been stable over a period (Home
Office, 1973a). Women are not greatly specialized as offenders,
they contribute to all categories of crime, but theirs are usually
minor, non-violent and they are rarely recidivists. In 1970 their
149,000 convictions were made up as shown in Table 4.1.

TABLE 4.1

43%	less serious motoring offences
15%	shoplifting
11%	other thefts
11%	failing to buy a wireless, car or dog licence
4%	drunkenness
1%	violent offences
15%	other offences

(Source: Home Office, 1971c)
The sex crime ratio varies considerably - there are about 4:1 male
to female convicted homicides, for robbery the ratio is nearer 50:1.
There are differences according to offence and age, women harm their
close relatives and friends (and themselves) and rarely attack out-
siders. Women have a double peaked curve of recorded offending,
reaching a high in adolescence and also in middle age and later.
Adulthood, marriage and responsibilities do not seem to 'cure' female crime as they do male and in old age there is one female convicted for every two males. In 1970, 26 per cent of female indictable offenders were over 40 compared with 11 per cent of the males.
On the whole, women commit very few serious crimes meriting long
sentences and their recidivism is confined to 'revolving door'
drunkenness and a few petty offenders. Fewer than 2 per cent of all
female offenders are sentenced to custodial care and only 3 per cent
of those convicted for indictable offences go to prison or borstal.

Even the indictable offences women commit are very petty: 90 per cent are property crimes and as a 1967 Home Office study shows, very trivial ones: 'A quarter of the offences involved goods valued at less than five shillings, over half less than £1. A fifth involved sums of £5 or more. A half involved thefts from self-service stores of which two-thirds were entirely of food'.

Social attitudes towards deviant females undoubtedly help to produce the low conviction rates. Conformity to fairly narrow role and class definitions in a society ensures that women produce and rear the next generation for that society. Differential attitudes towards deviant females appear to operate at at least three important levels in our social control process:

1 in early socialization when pressures and rewards for conforming behaviour are greater for girls;

2 in the scene-of-the-crime situation when female crime and deviance are more often 'contained' by communities and their agents of control: e.g. the police use cautions relatively more frequently for female than male offenders in relation to overall crime rates. 65,000:20,000 cautions for indictable offences in 1972. (The cautioning of prostitutes for soliciting under the 1959 Street Offences Act is a special and separate category here.) Thus, in Wilkins' terminology, female deviance is often 'modified' rather than amplified. In 'The Case of Mary Bell', Gitta Sereny describes how a family, friends, neighbours and other agencies did this, disastrously, for a mother and her daughter. Indeed, the concept of women, especially married women, as discrete, independent adults before the law is relatively novel: it is only about a century since wife chastisement became a crime and just half of one since a wife committing a felony in front of her husband was no longer presumed to be under his influence. Recent reports have shown that wifebeating remains a common occurrence and that interference from outside agencies, police, social workers or social security officers is only now becoming barely acceptable.

3 In court (and throughout disposal) women may be dealt with more leniently because their cases are so infrequent. A 1968 Home Office circular advises all courts to obtain social inquiry reports before sentencing any woman to imprisonment (although inquiry remands in custody may, paradoxically, therefore sometimes 'punish' women more) (Dell, 1971).

Although we may thus see that the deviance of women is less likely to develop into a secondary deviance pattern of a delinquent career with the stigma of imprisonment, a very small number of women still go to prison each year and a comparatively elaborate system exists to provide for them.

II   THE CONTEMPORARY SYSTEM

TABLE 4.2   Penal establishments for women in England and Wales

		Average daily population (1972)
Closed prisons	Holloway	305
	Styal (Cheshire)	183
Open prisons	Askham Grange (York)	86
	Moor Court (Stoke-on-Trent)	78
Remand centres	Low Newton (Durham)	19
	Pucklechurch (Bristol)	43
	Risley (Lancashire)	91
Closed borstals	Bullwood Hall (Essex)	108
	Holloway	15
	Styal	18
Open borstal	East Sutton Park (Kent)	34
	Total	980

(Source: Home Office, 1973b)

Research into female imprisonment in Britain has been very recent and very limited, so far; data on the inmate population is therefore scanty. Almost all of it is of the 'social arithmetic' kind, presenting simple statistical data on characteristics of offenders and from these one can derive a composite picture of women in prison. In addition, there are the personal and impressionistic accounts of ex-prisoners and staff; finally, there are a few serious studies of women's prisons, but these have been mainly done abroad.

Since the war, the average female prison population has varied between 800 and 1,000. Taking one year, 1970, there were 4,902 receptions of women and girls into penal establishments. It cannot be too strongly emphasized that most of these had not received sentences of imprisonment and were not subsequently so sentenced; they were either awaiting trial or reports before or after conviction. Of these, 1,674 were remanded in prison before trial, but not sent to prison.

1,029 were sent to prison for reports on conviction and then given a non-custodial sentence. In all, less than a quarter, 1,220, were sentenced to prison and these averaged $4\frac{1}{2}$ months each inside. 305 were sent to borstal (9 months on average). For those sentenced to prison, the largest offence group was property offences: 35 per cent, theft; 10 per cent, robbery and burglary; 9 per cent, fraud (Home Office, 1971b). Then 12 per cent were prostitution offenders, 11 per cent drinks or drugs offences; violence against other people amounted to 8 per cent. As already suggested, most sentenced-stays are short - 80 per cent are for under one year - and remands shorter still - a few weeks on average.

As to their characteristics, about two-thirds of those in prison

are under 40 (half under 25), but there is a small yet significant
older group, some in their 70s, many of whom have a drink problem.
Two surveys (in 1965 and 1967) suggest an alarming problem for the
children of some of the women in prison. In the 1965 study, 70 per
cent of convicted inmates had between them over 1,000 children,
mostly of a dependent age group (Home Office 1967). In 1971 Gibbs
found 35 per cent of the then Holloway sample had between them 2,000
dependent children of whom 1,000 had been living with their mothers
on arrest. Most women in prison are economically classified as
housewives or unemployed. Gibbens (1971), found many in the Holloway survey to be in poor health; 10 per cent had VD; mental ill-
health loomed even larger: 25 per cent had been in psychiatric
hospitals already, 20 per cent had made suicide attempts (50 per
cent of the drink and drugs group).

Women in prison are young or very old, very often unstable and
disturbed, and many have been institutionalized before. Their
offences have been fairly trivial, if repeated, and the costs borne
mostly by themselves and their young children. Of all those received in a year, most have been 'condemned' there before full trial
and sentence, after which they are released; of the quarter or so
who are sent back, most only serve very short sentences.

The consequences of this pattern for the prison system for women
can be readily perceived; prisons for women are notoriously difficult to run - while on the outside, women incur far fewer convictions than men and are much less prone to violence and aggression,
going to prison reverses this picture; twice the number of discipline offences are recorded against them and women are liable while
in prison to be more violent than their male counterparts (Home
Office, 1973b). Tension and hysteria are reported as frequent in
women's prisons - there are 'bang-ins' when locked in women hammer
on heating pipes, doors or walls, or 'smash-ins' when a woman or
group of women barricade themselves inside a cell and smash up the
furniture. Fights occur and so does self-mutilation with home-made
tattoos, wrist slashing, etc. Prison Department Reports since the
1960s have commented on difficulties with the increasingly disturbed
small group they have to deal with. But female establishments have
long reported problems of stability and control and several recent
studies have suggested that imprisoning women, given their social
role and their deviancy patterns, does create very special and distinctive difficulties.

III   The sociology of women's prisons

As discussed elsewhere in this volume, since the last war sociologists have contributed important analyses of total institutions and
especially (male) prisons, emphasizing inmate cultures and structures, and the impact of outside values on the prison. But only in
the mid-1960s were studies of women's prisons made and crucial differences observed in comparison with men's.

Ward and Kassebaum (1966) examined the California State Penitentiary for Women at Frontera while Giallombardo (1966) looked at the
State Women's Penitentiary at Alderson. These separate studies,
although differing on certain important issues, reached some

remarkably similar conclusions. For this discussion the most vital
of these were:
1   that women found the 'pains of imprisonment' much harder to bear
than men and this led
2   to the growth of a particular, compensatory inmate code and culture to ease these pains and that this, in turn, was
3   particularly mal-adaptive for rehabilitation.
    Men in prison lose freedom, good food and clothes, (hetero)sex,
autonomy and security; but they can still work, their 'outside'
status will be accorded them, and a politico-economic system functions in most male prisons to provide goods and services, activity
and role. Women 'outside' are expected to relate 'affectively' to
husbands and children and other family members. In prison they experience acute feelings of deprivation.
    In both US studies, as in the 1965 British survey, a high propor-
tion of women inmates had children - 68 per cent at Frontera. In
the USA children must normally be removed from their mothers into
care; in the UK mothers have been allowed to keep their babies with
them in closed prisons and borstals until the age of nine months;
more recently, older children stayed with their mothers in open
prisons up to two years of age. Prisons and borstals are hardly
ideal surroundings for infants and young children. There can have
been few grimmer sights in recent penal history than the yard at the
old Exeter mother and baby borstal (now transferred to Styal) where
a long row of babies in their prison prams sampled the fresh air of
one of our closed prisons as Judith Cook, a journalist, observed it
(1968), '"babies make such a difference"...lines of prams in the
exercise area and children crawling over the toys in the recreation
room...baby cots in prison cells and rows of prams outside prison
buildings....It is salutary to remember that being born in custody
did not go out with Dickens.'
    Imprisoned mothers, then, face a double dilemma: while men in
prison can to some extent assume that their wives are caring for the
family and will be receiving social security benefits, this is much
more difficult for lone fathers who are only rarely maintained as
full-time parents. So a wife loses her own central role and knows
that family life may be totally disrupted - 'problems of their children are more immediately acute' (Home Office, 1973b). For those
able to take their children into prison with them, or who give birth
to them there, other problems become acute: fears of the 'harm'
that the environment may do to them, anxieties about the 'unnatural'
way of life without fathers, siblings and an ordinary home.
    Loss of contact with their men worries many women prisoners and
it also adds to their role disorientation and fears. Ward and
Kassebaum found that 'absence of home and family' was the most difficult aspect of adjustment for almost half of their respondents;
as they point out, 'in a male dominated economic world, many women
obtain rewards or security by manipulating a man to provide them.
Penal confinement puts women entirely on their own without the complementary male roles with which they are actually or symbolically
aligned in the outside world.' They found (as did Giallombardo)
that the female inmate social code stresses the need to make a
'cool' adaptation by rejecting the outside world and concentrating
on inmate society until her 'time' is up.

As one girl put it, 'I couldn't come in off the streets, is the thing. You can do better time, if you just live in here and think about the things in here....But if you insist upon...wishing you were out there...you're gonna kill yourself. So when I finally decided to just forget all that out there for a while and give it a break and myself, I did better time' (Parker, 1965). Or Diane Richards, one of Tony Parker's 'Five Women' said, 'Prison's a world on its own, it's the only real world there is; you know that some day you're going to get out of it, but it's so far away it isn't worth thinking about....I just forgot the outside, I got on with doing it, it was me life, my whole life it was, for all of two years.'

So far, these adjustment problems may only seem acuter versions of those experienced by males. Yet, as already suggested, inmate life and social patterns in women's prisons are different and in unexpected ways: in prison, women are more violent than are men and not only are they personally violent but, in the Prison Department's words, '(a)...locked up...woman offender...resorts to expressing herself in action such as breaking glass or furniture, and sometimes assaulting officers or other inmates' (Home Office, 1973). Diane Richards again, 'Last August Bank Holiday all the girls on my land-ing we all went mad fighting and screaming and carrying on...we de-cided to barricade, we all got in my cell and we piled everything up against the door and then yelled at the screws to come and try to get us out. One of them they call Big Davies, she came along and started pushing at the door....We were all going mad, then more screws came along and they all got behind Big Davies and shoved and they all came tumbling in on top of us.' Men, on the other hand, (the troubles of 1972 being exceptional) are mainly reported for insubordination. Not only do women react more violently to impri-sonment but their subcultural adaptation also inverts outside values.

Both US studies found that the inmate social structures revolved round homosexual relationships. Giallombardo found the vast major-ity of inmates to be involved in these at Alderson, while at Fron-tera, 50 per cent were 'playing'. This compares with Clemmer's finding of 30 per cent male involvement in prison homosexuality. In both cases, the relationships were not simply for sexual satisfac-tion, but had a strong affectional and relational component. 'Affairs' were prolonged, complex and sentimental and involved il-licit note sending ('kiteing'), fights, and courtships. Most signi-ficant is the finding that while there was a small group of women who always played 'butch' roles (mostly lesbians outside) others were turnabouts who could be either passive or active in the same or in successive relationships. In other words, it was being in the relationship, rather than the physical satisfaction gained, which counted. Prison gossip, trade in goods and services, social status, all centred round the homosexual social network. Thus an interview with Ward went

Q. 'Do the women talk about homosexuality much?'
A. 'That's all they talk about. "Guess who's going with who?" and "They had a fight." O Jesus, that's all they talk about...because really, that's all that's happening here.'

Giallombardo adds an important contribution to these findings. She found that pseudo-families were erected on the basis of the

homosexual dyad and these extended to grandparents, siblings, etc.
This 'kinship' system, although loosely linked, formed the core of
community integration at Alderson and was vital to an understanding
of inmate roles. Although the type of participation in a sexual
alliance could vary, position in the family did not. While 'di-
vorce' was common, family breakdown was rare and family members were
mutually supportive. Assignment of roles, induction into roles and
thus into the prison itself were all achieved through the family.
These groups even marked off appropriate interaction partners; conversation with non-family members was frowned on. Eating together
and living together were appropriate too.

This further development of the homosexual subculture at Alderson
substantiates Ward and Kassebaum's view that the pattern at Frontera
was a response to the women's loss of their key affective and social
role, for Alderson was far more isolated than Frontera, the women
received almost no visits and their sentences (for Federal offences)
were much longer. Thus their pain-soothing adaptation was more elaborate and longer lasting, and more closely resembled, in its inver-
ted form, the family networks of the outside world.

If these networks solve the immediate problems of doing 'easy
time' for women, they do nothing to help them readapt after release.
In every sense, a women's prison is a more abnormal world than a
men's. Whereas large groups of men are confined together in military barracks, merchant ships, the fishing fleet, for long periods,
women are hardly ever grouped in all female institutions in our
society. Even convents have to have their male chaplains, doctors,
etc., while monasteries can be as divorced from femininity as those
Orthodox establishments where all domestic animals must be male too.
Not only are all female institutions much rarer in our society, but
the 'deviant' nature of them is further emphasized by the sex role
reversal in the staff hierarchy. Our society is man made and dominated. Power and authority figures are men and most women in
prison are or have been dependent upon them. Yet senior prison
staff are women and any male officers will be in subordinate positions as gate attendants and instructors. Women and girls in
British prisons and borstals are encouraged to work at a variety of
tasks - agriculture, bricklaying - which they may enjoy but which
'outside' they are debarred from as these are exclusively 'men's
work'. That they are so may be deplorable, but this does not help
the rehabilitation of the female offender in an unemancipated world.

The most marked inversion of the real world in the microcosm of
prison society lies, however, in the homosexual subculture. 'Outside', women are generally supposed to be less homosexual than men.
In fact, studies find most prison lesbians are 'jailhouse turnouts'
who go 'straight' outside, although for some, prison sex will have
been a disturbing experience.

'Once in a while you get somebody in here (Frontera) that cares
enough for you and they'll run for you on the outside, but that
doesn't happen very often. They get on the outside and forget about
this penitentiary and who's in here.' 'A disproportionately high
number of overt lesbians enter women's prisons - sometimes...in
Holloway all the crop-haired women in drag (make) you wonder...whe-
ther really you are in the Scrubs' (Pat Arrowsmith, 1969). The
fervid, intense relationships of prison life are thus of little

relevance to outside (although when they are, they will be beset by all the problems of ill-equipped women seeking economic indepen- dence) and simply make prison a little more bearable.

British establishments contain fewer women, mainly in for very short stays, and who have, in a small and homogenous country, better home contacts than their American counterparts. Applying these findings to Britain, where no such studies have been achieved, may not be valid. Yet our women's prisons are also characterized, by those who run them and those who join them, as hysterical, tense and violent. In recent times, lesbianism has been acknowledged as a 'problem', so there is probably some validity in these parallels.

IV   THE FUTURE

After the 1968 announcement of policy changes, the Home Office began the implementation of these by planning the rebuilding and reorien- tating of a 'new' Holloway on the old site. A series of policy documents present the case for this expensive and difficult (the old prison is still being used while the new one grows around it) pro- ject. From these statements, and others in recent official and related documents, two fundamental kinds of ambivalence towards the Holloway scheme in particular and female imprisonment in general appear. New Holloway is to be the showpiece and the pivot of the revamped female penal system. The old prison was condemned by everyone; deputy governor Mary Size called it this 'grim building'; it has been due for demolition since 1937. Faulkner in 1971 saw that 'the design of Holloway has come to be recognised as an ob- stacle to progress in the treatment of women offenders.'

Women offenders were seen as sick and in need of treatment: 'The outstanding feature of the description of the girls sentenced to borstal training or to detention in the detention centre is the large number of psychiatric cases sent to borstal where they can receive little treatment other than the sympathetic rapport, under- standing and guidance of the lay staff' (Goodman and Price, 1967). Gibbens found 20 per cent of his sample to have a 'major' mental health problem, and the Prison Department described 'the nature of the woman offender (as)...usually a disturbed, unhappy and frequent- ly inadequate personality.'

Dr Blyth, SMO at Holloway, described, in an address to the Howard League in January 1971, the elaborate plans for 'treatment' in the new Holloway. The whole ethos is to be therapeutic and means 'patients can be located in therapeutic groups instead of legal or imprisonment-term groups'. Facilities will be complex and treatment range from psychotropic drugs to deep analysis and group counsel- ling. Physically, the models suggest a modern shopping complex where security will be unobtrusive 'within the perimeter, the buil- dings will be grouped around a green to give an open aspect...while preserving a high degree of supervision' (Faulkner, 1971).

Plans for the New Holloway were launched with elaborate publicity early in 1972. Yet official ambivalence towards the project was also clear. Dr Blyth: 'if non-custodial treatment of women is to be undertaken, the New Holloway can be hived off to the NHS with pride' and 'It is a flexible unit and can be programmed to deal with

almost any demand upon it, even the physical assessment and treatment of prostitutes from without prison if brothels are legalised in
the future' (sic). Home Office publicity detailing the development
timetable describes the sophisticated and diverse therapies planned
for the New Holloway, including group therapy and counselling,
psycho drama and 'gymnastics...as a compensatory activity'. Splen-
did, no doubt, but each description is qualified by statements such
as 'can...only generally be applied to longer term prisoners';
'Sentences are not usually long enough for this form of treatment to
be effective'; ' 'only in the case of long term prisoners...will
psychiatric therapy be feasible.' But, as we have seen, and as the
report admits, a third of inmates will be on remand and ineligible
for treatment and the vast majority only serve short sentences. In
a 'New Society' article (25 February 1971) K. Fitzherbert said 'if
the new Holloway is completed in its projected form it will be a
study in ambiguity....The chief architect admits that he has been
advised to bear in mind that his building must, in no event, be obsolete if ever the day should come when women are no longer sentenced to prison.' Despite the carefully-contrived publicity, there
seems to be still a good deal of official ambiguity over the role of
the New Holloway as a women's prison and this reflects a more general policy - ambivalence towards the whole notion of imprisoning
women.

Reports, as I have suggested, have long stressed the problems of
managing and staffing women's prisons. Staffing is, in general, a
problem in all prisons, but women prison officers are in a somewhat
different situation from their male counterparts. As the Prison
Service recruits nationally and requires mobility for its staff it
creates difficulties for the married woman with a family and in the
past relied on single women. But with high marriage rates and early
marriage, single women have almost disappeared as a social phenomenon and most employers of teachers, social workers and clerical
staff have had to adapt accordingly. In fact, although the staffing
ratio in women's prisons is better than in men's (approximately 1:2
as against 1:3) it has worsened in recent years and of 500 female
officers in post in 1972 no fewer than 164 were temporary - a far
higher proportion than on the male side. Temporary staff are
usually locally recruited and not required to move about, and thus
these posts are obviously advantageous for many women. But this
expedient does not solve the acute problems. The proposed women's
wing at Grendon never materialized, apparently because of shortage
of appropriate staff. Plans for the New Holloway constantly stress
the need for more and better-qualified therapy-oriented staff, but
where and how they are to be recruited and retained is not clear.
Writing of her experience in F. Wing in 1969, Pat Arrowsmith said
'for a would-be therapeutic institution, Holloway is still lamenta-
bly short of psychiatric staff and social caseworkers...the wing
welfare worker is chronically overburdened.'

In some ways, this greater emphasis on therapy and welfare should
make the female officer's job a more attractive one. Certainly, the
pay, since it is equal to the men's, compares favourably with the
great inequalities outside, where women in industry only earn 60-70
per cent of a man's rate. The turnkey and discipline aspects are
much less emphasized and, indeed, British women's prisons employ men

staff on gate duty and to help handle violence: 'two or three men
officers...are called in from the gatehouse to help cope with anyone
who gets particularly unmanageable' (Buxton and Turner, 1962);   'if
a woman put in the "strips" refuses to undress and put on the...
canvas robe...the men come in and strip her themselves' (Pat Arrowsmith, 1969). Women officers are thus freer to concentrate on the
more 'feminine' role of rehabilitation and 'care'. But, with the
enormous expansion of social services today such opportunities for
'caring' work exist plentifully elsewhere and these need not generally entail custodial functions at all, nor involve weekend and
shift work. In practice, given the high proportion of remand-
receptions, the short sentences and the concentration of women in a
few institutions, remand centre staff in present undermanned establishments have little time for therapy work as they rush about on
ceaseless escort duties and complete the unending clerical work for
receptions, releases and transfers.

Staffing is thus a major difficulty in women's prisons and one
not likely to improve in the foreseeable future. Realization of
this central and intractable problem may be one reason why a more
generally ambivalent official attitude to female imprisonment has
become increasingly apparent. The curious case of the New Holloway
has already been outlined. But this view is wider.

It may well be that as the end of the century draws nearer,
penological progress will result in even fewer or no women at all
being given prison sentences. Other forms of penalty will be
devised which will reduce the number of women necessarily taken
from their homes, which so often ends in permanent disaster and
breakdown in family life (Home Office, 1970).

Lord Stonham while at the Home Office in 1970 felt that only a
few women need to be in prison: 'For a very few...security is the
main factor.'

Goodman and Price (now Davies) whose 1967 pamphlet, emphasizing
as it did the psychiatric needs of borstal girls, could have been
seen as support for more institutional therapy, note in their study
on girl offenders (Davies and Goodman, 1972)
    is it appropriate that the majority of 'non-psychiatric' girls
    should either be in prison or stay for at least six months in
    borstal?...is a long period in an all-Female institution likely
    to cure these (sex behaviour) problems? How much is the mental
    disturbance shown by these girls an initial reaction to incar-
    ceration?

Thus although a new and expensive women's prison is being built
with plans to run it in a radical way, increasing doubts emerge
about imprisoning women.

In summary, the picture we have built up of female imprisonment
helps to explain this duality. Historically, women have been imprisoned because men were and thus justice and the penal system
demanded it. But women in prison have always been troublesome and
their troubles and the general social view of appropriate treatment
have meant sensationalism and sentimentality. Authority has reacted
by either ignoring the different and special problems of women's
prisons or by introducing minor modifications of rules and regimes.
But, although there are many common problems and common sociological
features in men's and women's prisons, the differences are marked

and a valid basis for differential treatment can be argued.

Women officially offend very little. Only a tiny group are ever sent to prison. Of those who do, the majority will only be passing through and alternatives of bail hostels and non-custodial reporting agencies can easily be envisaged and arranged. The remainder are a minute slice of femininity with whom no one knows what to do. Whatever the good intentions, therapy and rehabilitation remain symbolic rather than actual goals because of staff shortages, lack of facilities, short sentences and the very smallness of numbers which makes provision of such facilities hardly seem worth while. Davies and Goodman (1972) point out that (of their sample)

a few (girls) enjoyed borstal...appearing to become over-dependent and slightly reluctant to face the outside community again....A greater number regarded borstal merely as a means of punishment and did not appreciate any aspect of it.

It is noteworthy that in several recent notorious cases, the prison authorities have implicitly announced the poverty of the female penal system, by sending these cases to male establishments. Finally, a much more general point must be made that we still know, intensive 'brain washing' apart, very little about how to change or modify people's behaviour, let alone how to do so with non-voluntary subjects, on a timetable predetermined elsewhere. 'Training' and 'treatment' must, then, remain as goals about which we still know far too little to achieve them confidently.

But, granted even adequate 'treatment' possibilities in a 'reasonable' environment, imprisoning women involves other problems which also, in any case, affect the possibility of treating them. As 'Treatment of Women and Girls in Custody' (Home Office, 1970), puts it: 'To send a woman to prison is to take her away from her family; the children in particular suffer from this deprivation which can lead to the break up of the home even where there is a stable marriage.' Prison deprives women of their usual social role; their response is often emotional, hysterical and violent, their solution an inversion of outside roles and values making rehabilitation even less attainable. Their children too are deprived, either inside in custody with their mothers or left behind in the outside world.

For a few high security risk women offenders, prison may continue to be the only 'solution' although the present female system cannot really cope with them now. For the rest, many alternatives have been proposed which take advantage of the low perceived social threat from female offenders. Official policy is already ambivalent about female imprisonment. A later edition of this chapter on the topic might well be merely an historical survey.

REFERENCES

ARROWSMITH, P. (1969), article in 'New Society', 4 September.
BLYTHE, R.K. (1971), 'New Plans for Treatment of Women and Girls', an address to the Howard League.
BUXTON, J. and TURNER, M. (1962), 'Gate Fever', The Cresset Press.
COOK, J. (1968), Born in Custody, 'Guardian', 30 October.
DAVIES, J. and GOODMAN, D. (1972), 'Girl Offenders aged 17 to 20

Years', Home Office Research Studies of Female Offenders, HMSO.
DELL, S. (1971), 'Silent in Court', G. Bell.
DU CANE, E. (1885), 'The Punishment and Prevention of Crime', Macmillan.
FAULKNER, D.E.R. (1971), The Redevelopment of Holloway Prison, 'Howard Journal', vol.13(2), pp.122-32.
GIALLOMBARDO, R. (1966), 'Society of Women', John Wiley.
GIBBENS, T.C.N. (1971), Female Offenders, 'British Journal of Hospital Medicine', September, vol.6(3), pp.279-82; 285-6.
GIBBS, C. (1971), The Effect of Imprisonment of Women on their Children, 'British Journal of Criminology', April, vol.2, pp.113-30.
GOODMAN, D. and PRICE, J. (1967), 'Studies of Female Offenders', Home Office Research Unit.
HANSARD (16 December 1968), H.C. Deb, vol.779, cols.206,307,308.
HOME OFFICE (1947), 'Report of the Commissioners of Prison and Directors of Convict Prisons for the Year 1945', HMSO.
HOME OFFICE (1967), 'Studies of Female Offenders' (Studies in the Causes of Delinquency and the Treatment of Offenders, no.11), HMSO.
HOME OFFICE (1970), 'Treatment of Women and Girls in Custody', HMSO.
HOME OFFICE (1971a), 'Report on the Work of the Prison Department 1970', HMSO, Cmnd 4806.
HOME OFFICE (1971b), 'Prison Department Report Statistical Tables', HMSO, Cmnd 5156.
HOME OFFICE (1971c), 'Criminal Statistics, England and Wales 1970', HMSO, Cmnd 4708.
HOME OFFICE (1973a), 'Criminal Statistics, England and Wales 1972', HMSO, Cmnd 5402.
HOME OFFICE (1973b), 'Report on the Work of the Prison Department 1972', HMSO, Cmnd 5375.
PARKER, T. (1965), 'Five Women', Hutchinson.
RUGGLES-BRISE, E. (1921), 'The English Prison System', Macmillan.
SERENY, G. (1972), 'The Case of Mary Bell', Eyre Methuen.
SMITH, A.D. (1962), 'Women in Prison, Stevens.
WARD, D.A. and KASSEBAUM, G. (1966), 'Women's Prisons', Weidenfeld & Nicholson.

Chapter 5

CUSTODIAL ALTERNATIVES

Hugh J. Klare

The tendency in England and Wales, as in other countries, is for custodial treatment to develop forms which are less custodial and which gradually come to resemble forms of treatment in the community which in turn involve a greater loss of freedom. Thus the pre-release employment scheme (PRES) involves residing in a prison hostel and working at an ordinary job in the community. A probation order with a requirement to reside at a probation hostel involves something very similar.

Whatever degree of liberty and choice is involved in such treatment forms as open institutions, outside working parties, home leaves or the pre-release employment scheme, they are all part and parcel of a custodial sentence. The courts cannot ensure that all or part of a custodial sentence is served in more or less open conditions. Technically, transfers to open conditions are a privilege, that is to say, an administrative device which may, or may not, be used and which may be revoked; all in accordance with criteria not known to the sentencer. Administratively, they are centrally organized.

By contrast, and quite apart from entirely voluntary treatment schemes which depend only on the willingness of the potential user to make use of the facilities offered (such as those at the experimental Barbican Centre in Gloucestershire), attendance at, say, one of the day training centres established under the Criminal Justice Act 1972 - a form of treatment in the community which involves some loss of freedom - is at present fixed by the sentencer. The regime at such centres is locally organized.

If the courts want to make sure, therefore, that treatment in the community is accompanied by close supervision and/or special treatment such as in- or out-patient psychiatric treatment, they must choose a community-based treatment form. Theoretically, there should also be some difference in personality between those offenders for whom complete loss of liberty, with only a possibility of greater freedom some time during their custodial sentence, appears appropriate; and other offenders for whom community-based treatment, admittedly with the certainty of some limited loss of freedom, seems right. Whether such differences exist in practice has not so far been established.

OPEN PRISONS

The first attempt to create an open institution within the English
prison and borstal system came in 1930 when some borstal lads were
taken on a march across the country from Feltham and started building Lowdham Grange in Nottinghamshire (Fox, 1952). This was certainly successful, in the sense that no one ran away on the way;
and also because it was a new departure, undertaken with considerable enthusiasm at the time when Paterson's approach seemed so hopeful and inspired many of the men personally picked by him, often as
house-master (i.e. assistant governors in borstals). It also demon-
strated that some of those sentenced to a custodial sentence could
be trusted, in conditions of near-freedom, not to abscond in significant numbers.

After the end of the 1939-45 war, the daily average prison
population which had been around 10,000 before the war, rose steeply
at a time of general austerity when little money was available for
general reconstruction, let alone the building of new penal institutions. As a result, a number of open prisons and borstals were set
up, not really as an expression of penal philosophy but as the
cheapest and easiest way of housing the growing number of inmates.
Nevertheless, this established open prisons as an institutional
treatment mode in its own right by demonstrating two things: one
was that not just a few but many prisoners could be trusted not to
run away; and second, that if a number did abscond, it did not
really matter all that much. Some were quickly caught, some returned of their own free will; but in any case no great harm was done
for those who escaped were a nuisance rather than a danger.

It did not, however, at that time occur to many people to wonder
how many offenders serving most or part of their prison sentence in
open conditions need not have had a custodial sentence at all. On
the contrary, symbolic steps in the opposite direction were often
taken by surrounding the institution, perhaps by a fence and a
manned gate which though it interposed a slight barrier between
outside and inside also became a psychological reminder that this
was indeed a prison.

There was no clear treatment rationale; no precise plans as to
what might conceivably be done with prisoners who have, say, difficulties in problem-solving or for others who are over-impulsive.
The main advantage that there was - and is - is that those pressures on individuals, prisoners and staff alike, which grow from the
feeling of being totally hemmed in, locked and blocked away from the
world, are felt less in open institutions. Moreover, the regime can
supply a valuable testing element, but there were - and are - also
disadvantages. Prisoners are mostly urban creatures. But open
prisons are sited in the countryside, many of them well away from
the beaten track. To the extent to which such institutions might be
used to attempt to reduce recidivism, perhaps through the acquisition of new and relevant social, technical or even academic skills,
existence so far away from family and neighbourhood and also from
the facilities of a city makes this rather difficult.

The use of open institutions was abruptly limited as a result of
the Mountbatten Report (Home Office, 1966) and all that surrounded
it. The appointment of Lord Mountbatten to inquire into security

arrangements in English prisons, finally triggered off by the escape
of Blake, the double agent, had been preceded by enormous publicity
about virtually all prison escapes towards the end of 1966.   Only a
few of these had been spectacular.   Many had been from the usual
outside working parties and open institutions where one or two week-
ly abscondings were normal.   By reporting all of these for a while
(and this despite the nearness of Christmas when more of what might
charitably be termed 'unauthorized home leaves' tended to occur
anyhow) the impression had been given that virtually any prisoner
could walk out of any prison with the greatest of ease.

How much of the avid, breathless and sometimes positively gleeful
reportage during this period, listened to and read just as avidly
and gleefully by the entire prison population, had itself contributed to further escapes is impossible to know.   The net result had
been a nervous and general reduction in any activities which could
conceivably be considered as entailing even a slight security risk.

The prison system has never been the same since.   Of course our
nineteenth-century prisons were not well designed to keep in custody
twentieth-century resourceful criminals serving long sentences.
But whether the sharp emphasis on widespread security, all the expenditure on costly electronic equipment, the need for more staff
and the diversion of part of it to pure security duties, dog handling, etc., was really worth it is another question.   Table 5.1
shows the number of escapes from prisons and remand centres (male
inmates only) during the last seven years for which statistics are
available, including the fateful 1966.

TABLE 5.1

	1966	1967	1968	1969	1970	1971	1972
Average population	25,461	26,909	24,712	26,886	30,468	31,274	30,274
Escapes from closed prisons and remand centres	79	23	21	33	39	38	77
Escapes from open prisons	278	203	213	261	235	219	194
Escapes from escorts and supervised outside work-ing parties	163	75	65	97	101	107	85

It will be seen that the number of escapes from closed prisons in
1972 was almost as high as in the immediate pre-Mountbatten year.
Admittedly the total average prison population for 1972 was higher
than in 1966.   Also throughout the six post-Mountbatten years, the
number of escapes from special security wings or dispersal prisons

was tiny, and in some years it was nil. Perfect security is, however, impossible to attain; and high security has a very restricting effect on dispersal prisons. The number of escapes from open
prisons has certainly been reduced; but so has the number of those
actually held in such institutions. The cost of somewhat greater
security has been high, both economically and in terms of the atmosphere and regime in prisons generally.

The Report of the Prison Department for 1972 shows 12 open training prisons for men, able to accommodate 4,216 prisoners but with a
daily average population of only 3,578. In addition, 12 open borstals for young male offenders with a capacity of 2,229 had an
average population of only 1,797. There are also two open prisons
for women (capacity of 191, daily average population 164) and an
open borstal for girls (capacity 231, daily average population 175).

One of the other consequences of the Mountbatten Report was the
introduction of a new system of security categorization of prisoners - ranging from A (high risk) to D (minimum risk). For men at
any rate, only category D prisoners are eligible for open prisons
and clearly the prison administration feels that not enough men can
be placed into this category to take up all the places in open institutions. It may also be that the existence of parole means that
some men serving sentences of between eighteen months and five years
who might otherwise have been reclassified category D towards the
middle of their sentence are now released on licence and therefore
never reach open prisons.

The work which open prisons provide is mostly outdoors, healthy
enough for city dwellers but not always particularly relevant either
to the problems of individual prisoners or to whatever work those
discharged are likely to attempt. By the end of 1972, about 11,000
acres of land were being farmed and this resulted in produce worth
over £$\frac{1}{2}$ million. This is quite a useful amount to offset against
the enormous cost of the prison system. But prison labour is expensive, even in open prisons and the 11,000 acres could probably have
been farmed more cheaply in other ways.

As far as the general regime is concerned, the original attempt
to copy or adapt the atmosphere of the public school has on the
whole been abandoned. The prison rules, originally framed for
closed prisons, apply also to open institutions and act as a con-
straint (but in practice modifications occur, e.g. visiting arrangements are usually more generous). There is often a fair degree of
inmate participation in various aspects of the life of such institutions and many more opportunities to voice criticisms verbally than
in closed prisons. One or two of the magazines which are published
in open institutions can be quite sharp on occasions. This is
healthy because it provides an outlet for dissent and frustrations
and also sometimes for the expression of critical, honest, non-con-
formist but non-criminal attitudes. This is a great rarity in the
artificial world of any prison, normally so full of stereotypes and
all kinds of fantasies and make-believe.

When such frankness occurs in open prisons (as it does in Grendon) it is perhaps particularly relevant for their population. The
medium and long-term open institutions contain more than the average
proportion of passive, conforming but sometimes highly devious and
secretive individuals - con-men, fraudsters, defaulting solicitors,

potential bowler hat wearers of all sorts who do their sometimes considerable damage beneath a facade of rigid respectability. The open
expression of criticism, self-criticism and honest dissent may hopefully provide a learning experience for such individuals; though
sometimes their inner confidence and sense of self-hood is so shaky
that a false identity, overtly reinforcing conformist values while
secretly undermining them, is the only way they dare survive.

There is also more interplay between an open institution and its
surrounding community than there could ever be in the life of a
maximum security prison and that of its neighbourhood. But their
sites limit the kind of interaction that can take place and under-
lines how different life is in the country from the existence in
towns and cities to which so many prisoners return.

Open institutions also help to enrich the experience of at least
some members of the prison service. If there were to be a service
for closed prisons only, it would be even more inward-looking than
it is. Basic-grade officers - the bulk of the prison service - get
less chance of a variety of experiences since, once they are in
post, they tend to stay there and usually only move on promotion.
But assistant governors and governors move frequently - too frequently, in fact, for them to enable what might be a promising experiment in treatment to be sustained without great difficulty.

Moreover, open prisons are relatively small and the top jobs are
only graded governors III or II. This is not to argue that the top
jobs in large maximum security or dispersal prisons should not
carry the rank of governor I. Rather is it the old complaint that
promotion should not only be tied to easily measurable criteria such
as, for example, the number of inmates and staff but also take into
account special social skills. It would be desirable that particularly able governors running an open prison, or indeed any other
institution, could be promoted in situ, so that a special regime or
experiment could be continued more easily.

It may be argued - and no doubt has been inside Civil Service
establishment departments - that special social skills are difficult
to assess. To this it may be replied that the National Health Service uses a system of merit awards for medical consultants and if it
is really too complicated to promote on the basis of special social
skill (general social skills are essential in the management of all
prisons), a case could be made out for merit awards for governors.
It is important, however, that such awards should also be reflected
in terms of pension rights so that a governor who believes he should
see an experiment through for an adequate period is not penalized
when he retires.

Not all governors will want to stay in one particular prison for
longer than the usual three years. In planning the careers of
governors and, for that matter, of uniformed staff, careful consideration should be given to precisely when experience in open institutions is most helpful to the individual in question. This is
already done to some extent; but the service is under such pressure
that the effectiveness of career planning is not yet what it ought
to be.

The siting of one of the prison officer training schools at
Leyhill open prison is entirely desirable. It could be particularly
useful for officers on 'development' or other refresher courses who

have served for some time in a closed prison, if more use of it were
made for them, to experience the atmosphere of an open institution
and to be able to have informal talks to the different members of
the staff there. This and various secondments to outside agencies
such as probation offices, social service departments and voluntary
agencies, unhappily now restricted, are essential if the inevitable
institutionalization of prison officers is to be counteracted.

OUTSIDE WORKING PARTIES

These are groups of prisoners who leave the institution in the morn-
ing and return to it in the afternoons, having undertaken some
specific job, perhaps working on the road, undertaking repairs or
decoration or even going to another prison not too far away to work
there. Usually such working parties are under the supervision of
prison officers and, as Table 5.1 shows, escapes from escort and
from supervised working parties have fallen fairly steeply. How
these figures are divided between escorts and working parties cannot be established but of course tighter security measures have also
been applied to all of these since 1966 - presumably more stringent-
ly so to escorts to and from courts.
    The value of such working parties has usually been simply to
break up the monotony of life for prisoners who are not high security risks. There are also unsupervised working parties, traditionally small individual jobs such as doing a bit of gardening for
someone. But recently work of a different nature in which inmates -
normally from borstals - could see themselves clearly in a helping
role has been undertaken. One of the more recent of such schemes is
being run in conjunction with Community Service Volunteers. According to this, selected young men are placed in residential projects
such as in mental hospitals, schools for maladjusted or physically
handicapped children or in one of the Cheshire Homes for a period of
up to 28 days, usually in the month just before their discharge.
Though the placement is inspected beforehand, perhaps by an assistant governor, and visited while the work is going on, it is otherwise unsupervised by prison staff.
    Projects devised in the community itself, sometimes as an alter-
native to a custodial sentence, can take this idea much further and
can provide training for selected ex-offenders to work in areas of
special social need - as for example the New Careers schemes in
California and, more recently, in Bristol.

PRE-RELEASE EMPLOYMENT SCHEME

This involves the placement of prisoners in a prison hostel during
the last few months of his prison sentence but before his normal
date of release which - if no remission has been lost - is after two-
thirds of the sentence have been served in custody unless a period
of parole is granted. The idea of the scheme is to get prisoners
used to life outside, to work in factories or offices, in short to
get them de-institutionalized after what may have been a substantial
period inside.

For men, nine of the larger local prisons, five closed training prisons and two open prisons run pre-release employment schemes. Hollesley Bay open borstal for young men, Askham Grange open prison for women and two borstals for girls, Bullwood Hall (closed) and East Sutton Park (open) also operate pre-release hostels. But recently unemployment has cut down the number of jobs in the areas where there are pre-release units and also seems to have made employers more reluctant to take on prisoners rather than others who need work (Home Office, 1973). Nevertheless, 656 men went on pre-release schemes in 1972 and many completed it successfully. A few committed serious offences while on the scheme, however.

Sometimes the successful completion of a pre-release employment scheme is envisaged by the Parole Board as a preliminary to parole. Strangely enough the Parole Board does not, so far, know the precise criteria for selection for PRES (recently re-examined and probably tightened) nor can it make the scheme a pre-condition for parole. But sometimes a parole dossier may indicate that a prisoner has already been recommended for PRES. In such a case, it has happened that the Board prefers the PRES to a short period of ordinary parole.

HOME LEAVES AND CONJUGAL VISITS

At present prisoners serving three years or more are eligible to two periods of home leave, one over a weekend ('short home leave') and a longer one lasting five days. This latter, fearsomely named 'terminal home leave', may be taken about nine months before discharge from prison. Home leaves enable a prisoner to make contact with his family and friends and perhaps to have interviews for jobs. Homeless men may spend their leaves in a hostel if a suitable vacancy can be found.

In Sweden, home leaves or 'furloughs' are granted much more frequently, often at regular intervals throughout the sentence, except for maximum security prisoners. The results have been good since morale amongst prisoners has improved and the system has not been abused. A similar extension of home leave should at least be tried out in this country to see how it works and in what way it can best be administered. Sweden also has a special prison where long-term prisoners can have a 'holiday' with their wives and families. The prison is secure but internal security is not very intrusive since the number there at any one time is always small. There are leisure activities and play facilities for the children.

Finally, Sweden also has a system of conjugal visits. Wives and girl-friends may visit prisoners and stay with them in their cells which may be locked from the inside. The pros, e.g. relief of sexual tensions (Eleventh Report of the Estimates Committee, 1966-7), and cons, e.g. frustration because of unsatisfactory sexual relations in off-putting surroundings or because they were too eagerly awaited (Home Office, 1968) of this have been discussed in two official reports. What may be added is that whenever a relationship is involved that has lasted in the past (whether with a wife or common-law wife) more is needed to maintain it than a short visit, whether or not sexual intercourse is a part of such a visit. It takes time to have a proper row, let alone a real reconciliation

and it takes more time to adjust to a situation which remains static
for the prisoner but may change considerably for the woman concerned
(or man if the prisoner is a woman) who may have had to shoulder entirely new responsibilities and deal with quite new problems.
'Fings', to quote Frank Norman's highly appropriate title, 'ain't
wot they used to be.'

If a system of regular home leaves were introduced for all prisoners except those in category A, this would also reduce the need
for conjugal visits. But clearly different arrangements would have
to be made for category A prisoners, who cannot be released on home
leave, if both they and their families wish to maintain their domestic ties. There is a good case to be made out for having a few
flats inside some of the dispersal prisons where wives and children
may come for a weekend. The children would need room to play as
well as time to get used to their father again; and the prison
welfare officer might usefully get involved in whatever family problems might arise before, during or after such weekend visits.
Women prison officers would no doubt have to carry out careful
searches of wives and families before and after such weekend visits.
There are very few top security women prisoners but if they had husbands and families similar arrangements should be envisaged.

INTERMITTENT CUSTODY

This is a form of custodial treatment the aim of which is frankly
deterrent. In this country, it may be said that attendance centres
belong to this category. Attendance at such centres involve the
regular loss of a few hours of leisure time at weekends over a
specified number of weeks which the young offenders concerned spend
in compulsory but more or less irrelevant activities. Attendance
centres are not part of the central prison system but are organized
and staffed locally and may vary from place to place. Valiant
attempts are made to fill the hours with some activity, usually of
the physical kind, which might at least make the time and effort
concerned seem a little more meaningful, if only to the staff.

Various forms of intermittent custody have been tried in European countries, including the concept of weekend prisons. All kinds
of efforts have been made to delineate categories of offenders for
whom this form of custodial treatment might be appropriate. It was
thought, for example, that it might be right for motoring offenders
who could keep their jobs during the week and serve their sentence
at weekends. But this notion may have been based on early stereo-
typed ideas of motoring offenders as largely middle-class, middle-
aged executives who could cope easily with fines and for whom a bit
of compulsory log-felling at the weekend might be just the thing.
But in practice it is not easy to find sufficient offenders for whom
such a sentence might be appropriate (Willet, 1964).

Even if they did serve a useful purpose, weekend prisons, as part
of our central prison system (as they are in other countries), would
be difficult to organize here since, apart from the general shortage
of prison staff, officers do not want to work at weekends if it can
possibly be avoided. Nor would it be easy to organize even faintly
meaningful but spasmodic short-term activities for the offenders
concerned.

Something may be said, however, for non-custodial weekend or evening activities or even for the intermittent use of some special facility which may be provided in a prison: for example by way of continuing regular psychotherapeutic sessions when a relationship has been established while a sentence is being served. The new Holloway prison provides for out-patient facilities and there is no reason why these should only be used for women and girls on remand; and not also for those who would benefit from the continuation of treatment which was begun inside. Intermittent attendance at such clinics during the day or in the evenings could be voluntary or as a requirement of a probation order.

THE FUTURE

Over the last twenty years, the number of custodial sentences has fallen considerably, from 440 per 1,000 persons convicted in England and Wales in 1953 to 197 in 1972. The actual average prison population also declined from the all-time high of 39,700 in 1971 to about 36,000 in March 1974. This trend ought to be accelerated further. One way of doing so would be to release all category D prisoners after a third of their sentence had been served. This proposal ties in with some of the recommendations made during the 1973 Cropwood Conference on parole (Hood, 1973) and with the Prison Department's own perception of category D prisoners as being those inmates who constitute the least danger to the public.

The great majority of these are inadequate petty offenders who ought not to be given prison sentences at all, but who might be much better dealt with by intensive help in the community. Of course, it will take time to establish such community projects in sufficient numbers. Meanwhile, however, the shorter a time category D prisoners are kept inside the better. If the courts believe that deterrence could appropriately play a part in the sentence for such offenders, and if they feel experience of prison might provide this, then even a brief period inside would be sufficient. Longer in such cases is likely to be counter-productive.

At present, most open prisons are precisely for category D prisoners. In future, if the number of category D prisoners is reduced, open institutions could be used for three purposes. The first of these would be as an intermediate stage between maximum security and freedom for former top security prisoners as they get nearer to their release, whether on parole or otherwise; and especially if no suitable pre-release employment schemes can be arranged.

The second would be as middle-term prisons for category B and C prisoners. It is at least worth trying such a much bolder policy. It may well demonstrate - just as the original North Sea Camp did - that what was unthinkable yesterday becomes feasible tomorrow.

Finally the third use would be, as it is now, for detaining certain types of prisoners for whom a long sentence is inevitable - major fraudsters and some murderers, for example - but who are nevertheless known to be good security risks.

REFERENCES

Eleventh Report of the Estimates Committee, Parliamentary Session, 1966-7, 'Prisons, Borstals and Detention Centres', HMSO, HCP 599.
FOX, L.W. (1952), 'The English Prison and Borstal Systems', Routledge & Kegan Paul.
HOME OFFICE (1966), 'Report of the Inquiry into Prison Escapes and Security by Admiral of the Fleet Earl Mountbatten of Burma', HMSO, Cmnd 3175 ('Mountbatten Report').
HOME OFFICE (1968), 'The Regime for Long-term Prisoners in Conditions of Maximum Security', Report of the Advisory Council on the Penal System, HMSO ('Radzinowicz Report').
HOME OFFICE (1973), 'Report on the Work of the Prison Department, 1972', HMSO, Cmnd 5375.
HOOD, R.G. (1973), 'Some Fundamental Dilemmas of the English Parole System and a Suggestion for an Alternative Structure', paper given at Cropwood Round-table Conference on Parole, Cambridge.
WILLET, T.C. (1964), 'Criminal on the Road', Tavistock.

Chapter 6

ALTERNATIVES TO IMPRISONMENT

Keith Hawkins

We suspect that it passes the wit of man to contrive a prison
which shall not be gravely injurious to the minds of the vast
majority of prisoners, if not also to their bodies. So far as
can be seen at present, the most practical and hopeful of
'prison reforms' is to keep people out of prison altogether!
(S. and B. Webb, 1922, p.248)

I

For most people prison symbolizes the penal system; and for more
than a century, following the decline in the use of capital punishment and the demise of transportation, prison has stood at the heart
of English penal practice. But times change. The social and economic setting of the penal system is continually shifting. Public
attitudes to crime and punishment imperceptibly alter. Even Lord
Justice Lawton, the son of a prison governor, and a judge who is not
known for excessive leniency when sentencing offenders, has said
that loss of liberty 'is an inappropriate, useless and expensive
sanction for approximately three-quarters of those who now find
themselves in custody.' Official statements of penal policy, if
less bluntly expressed, also reveal a disenchantment with imprisonment. Referring to 'many' who have to be confined a Government
White Paper has said
> Long periods in prison may punish, or possibly deter them, but do
> them no good - certainly do not fit them for re-entry into soci-
> ety. Every additional year of prison progressively unfits them
> (Home Office, 1965, para. 3).

Throughout this century the application of imprisonment has been
restricted and its character changed substantially. It has come to
be seen as undesirable for certain groups (the young, for example,
and most first offenders), while others, such as the mentally disturbed, have been redefined as cases falling more in the province of
social welfare for whom prison is equally unsuitable. Having been a
relative commonplace in the penal system imprisonment is now the
most drastic sanction for deviant behaviour. The dissatisfaction
with imprisonment and its damaging after-effects has motivated a

search for alternative penalties which would restrict its application either by dealing with offenders by methods short of imprisonment or by releasing them from prison earlier than they would
otherwise have been. For others who have continued to be confined,
a wider variety of institutions and regimes have made imprisonment
itself more flexible and diverse. Hostel schemes have been developed, for example, and since the war about 4,000 places have become
available in open prisons, and for the future suggestions have been
heard about the introduction of some form of intermittent custody
such as weekend detention.

The purpose of this essay is to consider some of the pressures
which have dictated the search for alternatives to imprisonment for
sentenced adult prisoners and to discuss some of the implications of
this shift in emphasis. (1) This is not the place, however, either
to discuss why the non-custodial measures which have been developed
have taken the particular form that they have, (2) or to rehearse in
detail their legal and administrative provisions. (These are covered in the various textbooks on the penal system: see, for example, McClean and Wood, 1969; Walker, 1968; and Hall Williams,
1970).

II

The development of alternatives to imprisonment, it seems, has been
promoted more by a variety of pressures on the penal system than by
an independent analysis of problems of penal policy. This is a complex process and though it is impossible here to disentangle the
various strands of influence which have shaped the system, it is
possible to point to some of the forces which have brought change.
The first of these is humanitarianism. It is a commonplace to
observe that social attitudes as to the appropriateness of various
punishments have changed dramatically in the last century and a
half. The penal system has become more benevolent as a result of
the concern to mitigate unnecessary cruelty or harshness (3) in the
treatment of offenders and a desire to establish basic standards of
propriety and decency. Except for latterday overcrowding there has
been a general improvement in prison conditions - fewer indignities,
a less spartan regime, better food, the abolition of hard, unproduc-
tive labour, and a strengthening of the contact between prisoners
and the outside world.

Second, owing to the growth of social and behavioural sciences
people have come to see offenders in a different light. The classi-
cal conception which stressed that the punishment fit the crime was
predominant when prison emerged as the chief method of disposal.
Gradually, however, there developed the beginnings of intellectual
curiosity in the origins of criminal behaviour. Though there were
often substantial differences in the interpretations which were
offered, they did share the common foundation of determinism. It
had a strong influence on general penal policy and on the character
of imprisonment, but made less impact on sentencing policy. So far
as penal theory was concerned the aim became no longer to fit the
punishment to the crime but to fit the treatment to the offender, no
longer to deal with him for what he had done so much as for what had

become, no longer to punish, but to rehabilitate. To rectify what
appeared to be the basic problems causing criminality required (in
theory) not a simple, undifferentiated approach, but treatment and
training adapted to each individual and administered by specially-
trained personnel. When offenders' needs as well as their deserts
have to be catered for, it is easier to see imprisonment as unsuitable for the rehabilitation of a large group of offenders. In England this change in emphasis was most marked by the development of
probation and borstal, in the United States by probation, parole,
the indeterminate sentence and the Reformatory.

     Rehabilitating offenders has been officially considered the pri-
mary aim of the penal system in England since the report of the
Gladstone Committee in 1895 (though it is clear that other aims have
not been put aside - especially by the courts in fixing sentence).
As soon as rehabilitation is admitted as a formal aim of a penal
system, however, the place and worth of imprisonment stands on sha-
kier ground. It is possible to justify prison as a means of exact-
ing retribution, of reflecting the condemnation of the community for
the criminal act, of incapacitating offenders for a certain period
of time, perhaps even of deterring others who might also be tempted.
But to say, as does the first of the Prison Rules, that the purpose
of the training and treatment of convicted prisoners shall be to
encourage and assist them to lead a good and useful life opens the
way for a wide variety of criticisms. These are well known and need
only brief discussion.

     The architecture of most English prisons reveals purposes in
penal policy other than the rehabilitation of offenders: imprisonment purports to reform offenders even though reform is usually to
be accomplished in a nineteenth century setting. Of greater importance, however, is a fundamental contradiction, if one holds to a
deterministic criminology, in professing to change offenders to live
at liberty without breaking the law by training them behind bars.
But the primary emphases of any prison regime have to be security
and control since these are fundamental to any other aims. The
stricter the control, the more mindless the discipline, the greater
the dependence inculcated. It is a familiar comment that 'every
year of prison progressively unfits a man for re-entry into the
community'. (Most of the aphorisms of penology are concerned with
prison.) Furthermore, there are two major assumptions involved:
that prisoners perceive themselves as in need of treatment or training, and that prison staffs share the official aim. Imprisonment
also severs links with the community; it ruptures the major stabi-
lizing influences - family, job and friends. Far from reintegrating
offenders, it is widely accepted that prison isolates. To imprison
an individual is to risk embittering him. It is to risk the con-
taminating effects of the enforced intimate contact with other offenders which may transmit pro-criminal values, knowledge and techniques. It is also to force him to bear the stigma of prison which,
whatever its impact on his self-image, is likely to obstruct or
destroy the chance of reacceptance by family, friends and employers.
Even though statistics show that a large proportion of those sent to
prison for the first time do not return to prison, many commentators
feel that this result is bought at too high a price, especially as
similar results are achieved with non-custodial measures. Certainly

evaluative research challenges the optimistic assumptions of those who advocate a rehabilitative prison regime. At the same time the efficacy of the other major utilitarian aim - deterrence - is also being seriously questioned. The upshot of all this is a disillusionment about the effectiveness of imprisonment as a means of accomplishing anything apart from punishment or incapacitation. 'The most that can be done in the traditional institution', Conrad has said, 'is to maintain order' (1965, p.292).

Another very different kind of influence on the development of penal systems is the number of offenders to be dealt with. Prisons are apt to become overcrowded. Official statements show considerable concern for this problem:

Overcrowding is the worst feature of our prison system, worse even than the old buildings in which it takes place, and its effects are seen throughout the system. (Home Office, 1969, para. 239)

When prisons are overcrowded it is more difficult to claim that their inmates are undergoing rehabilitative treatment and training. It is more difficult even to carry out the first task of imprisonment, that of control:

Overcrowding weakens security and makes it more difficult for staff to get to know prisoners. (Home Office, 1969, para. 239)

Overcrowded prisons tend to generate tension among the inmates and make for other administrative problems. They also give rise to offensive living conditions. Even prosaic matters assume great importance in these circumstances:

it is not so easy, though it has to be done, to overcrowd men in workshops, to produce more meals from the same kitchens, to give more men baths in old bath houses, or to supervise more visits in the same visiting room. (Home Office, 1969), para. 239)

Since overcrowding places severe stress on resources those who advocate the use of alternatives to imprisonment can also argue that there is a better chance of dealing effectively with those who have to be kept in secure conditions if numbers are reduced.

Lastly, economic motives also prompt innovation. One of the reasons in the past for the popularity of probation, for example, has been its low cost (Mannheim, 1939, p.55).

Imprisonment is not only inappropriate and harmful for many offenders for whom it is used; often it is also a wasteful use of limited resources. Cost is not the only factor, but it is worth observing that, quite apart from the increased risk that the State would have to support the family of an offender deprived of liberty, the cost of maintaining an inmate in a prison service establishment is on the average about £22 a week. No official estimate has been made of the average cost of supervising a probationer but we would judge it to be of the order of £1 a week. (Home Office, 1970, para. 9)

The economics of the penal system are now assuming much greater importance. Traditionally penal measures have been evaluated in terms of their apparent impact, if any, on the behaviour of offenders under study; they have not usually been evaluated in cost-benefit terms. There are some exceptions, however, mainly in California, a state which for some time has been politically sensitive to public expenditure. (4) The Probation Subsidy Program in

California illustrates how change in penal practice can be stimula-
ted by the recognition that imprisonment is a costly business. This
Program was based on the following assumptions:
  (1) probation is one of the least costly correctional services
  currently available;
  (2) for a large number of cases, probation is at least as effective, as most institutional forms of correctional care; and
  (3) (the rate at which probation is granted) could be increased
  without substantially increasing the rate of violation among
  probationers. (Smith, 1968, p.4)
Probation is administered by the counties in California, in contrast
with the prisons which are the responsibility of the state administration. The basic principle of the Program is that the counties
are encouraged to improve the quality of their probation services
and at the same time the state pays the counties for results achieved in proportion to their success (Smith, 1967, p.12). In the
political climate which emphasized restricted state expenditure the
courts were given clear encouragement to keep people out of the
state prisons. For every offender put on probation who would otherwise have been committed to prison, the county authorities received
a subsidy of 4,000 dollars, a sum capable of supporting six to eight
people under special probation supervision. The result was a sometimes striking increase in the numbers of those put on probation and
a decline in the population levels in the prisons despite a slight
increase in terms served. Summing up the first two years' experience of the Program, Robert L. Smith writes:
  Since July 1, 1966, 3928 people who might otherwise have come
  into the state correctional systems have been diverted from _ .
  Construction of institutional beds to accommodate these peopl :
  (at 20,000 dollars per new bed) would have cost approximately
  78 million dollars. On the basis of a minimum cost of 4,000
  dollars per individual criminal career, these new cases could
  have cost the state 15.7 million dollars; the actual cost
  through subsidy is only 5 million reimbursement dollars for these
  same cases during the first two-year period. (1968, p.5)
And one of the probation departments reported of its first year's
experience:
  The special supervision program has been financially profitable
  to both the county and the state. Our county invested approximately 70,000 dollars of new money in the program; in return, it
  earned 164,000 dollars. In terms of criminal career cost to the
  state, it is clear that the state and the county have benefited
  financially. (Smith, 1967, p.13)
Probation, in other words, was extended and developed and became a
more attractive proposition for the courts, not simply because they
felt it to be a more suitable form of treating and training offenders than imprisonment, but because of the money saved. (5)

III

In studying the evolution of alternatives to imprisonment in England, one is led to the conclusion that at present expediency and
economy largely influence that which is interpreted as desirable

penal policy. To some extent this proposition may be illustrated
by looking briefly at the background to recent English legislation
affecting imprisonment. 'Two factors have dominated the history of
the prison service ever since the war', a Government White Paper
has said. 'The first is the rise in numbers, and the consequent
overcrowding. The second is the development of alternatives to the
traditional form of imprisonment' (Home Office, 1969, para. 237).
(6)

The Criminal Justice Bill of 1938 is a useful point of departure
since its mark remains on much of the present English penal system.
According to Sir Samuel Hoare, the Bill was founded on two broad
principles; that 'undue severity, quite apart from its brutalising
effect, is an unsuccessful way of dealing with crime', and that 'you
cannot deal with crime and criminals by any rough-and-ready method'
(H.C. Deb. (342) col. 270). The Bill was not especially ambitious
in attempting to restrict the use of imprisonment, being confined
largely to young offenders. The Home Secretary offered conventional
arguments, considering prison to be 'the worst possible way of dealing with these uncontrolled, objectionable and sometimes dangerous
young people.' 'Prison', he went on, 'particularly after a short
sentence, often turns them into little heroes. It makes a dangerous
break in the thread of their lives. It gives them no training for
the future....It often destroys any deterrent effect that imprisonment may have' (col. 272).

Though this Bill came to nothing owing to the outbreak of war, it
was revived in a modified form in 1947. By this time, however,
there had been a dramatic increase in the prison population. The
daily average population in 1938 had been 11,086, but by 1945 it had
risen to 14,708 in spite of an increase in remission from one-sixth
to one-third which had come into effect during the war (Rose, 1961,
p.239). The post-war Parliamentary Debates reveal a firmer deter-
mination to restrict the imprisonment of young people. Chuter Ede,
the Home Secretary, spoke of the 'evil which ought to be avoided,
unless there is no possible alternative' (H.C. Deb. (449) col.
1309). (7) And the criticism that imprisonment might contaminate -
not heard in 1938 - was voiced (H.C. Deb. (444) col. 2136 (Hoare);
H.L. Deb. (155) col. 392 (Jowitt)). Thus following the 1948 Act,
magistrates' courts could no longer impose a sentence of imprisonment on those under seventeen years of age and the higher courts
those under fifteen (S. 17(1)). The Act also tried to persuade
sentencers not to imprison those under twenty-one, forbidding it
unless they were of the opinion that no other method of dealing with
them was appropriate (S. 17(2)). (8)

To restrict the use of imprisonment, however, was not enough.
Attractive alternatives had to be devised: this meant making the
penal system more flexible. Chuter Ede spoke of the aim in the Bill
of providing the authorities,

> both the courts and those who are responsible for the custody of
> convicted persons, means by which a greater variety of treatment
> of the individual is available, so that the treatment of the
> offender can be decided with reference to all the circumstances
> of his individual case. (H.C. Deb. (449) cols 1308-9)

The Act accordingly emphasized the desirability of using non-custodial methods for adults. It amended the use of probation (ss. 3-6),

made formal provision for the courts to grant absolute or condition-
al discharge (s. 7) and gave the power to impose a fine for any
offence except in those very exceptional cases where the penalty is
fixed by law (s. 13). (9)

Between the major Criminal Justice Acts of 1948 and 1967 comes a
minor but interesting piece of legislation: the First Offenders Act
1958. (10) Following a recommendation made by the Advisory Council
on the Treatment of Offenders in its report on 'Alternatives to
Short Terms of Imprisonment' (Home Office, 1957, paras 53-6), this
Act adopted for adults the approach to the restriction of imprisonment of young offenders made by s. 17 of the 1948 Act. This section
was generally believed to have been very successful and there was
little opposition in Parliament to an extension of the principle.
Sir George Benson enthusiastically described the effect of s. 17 as
'spectacular'.

> Instantaneously, it reduced the number of adolescents sent to
> prison by one-half, and for the last eight years the figure for
> imprisonment of adolescents has remained one-half of what it was
> before the Criminal Justice Act was passed. (H.C. Deb. (582)
> col. 399)

There had been a sharp increase in the prison population in the
mid1950s and the First Offenders Act was passed at a time when the
population of offenders in prisons and borstals was the highest
ever recorded. Overcrowding focused attention in Parliament on
issues which had not been explicitly recognized before. The pre-
occupation of those who spoke in the Debates on the Bill is clear:
it was not the harmful effects of imprisonment nor the erosion of
the deterrent power of prison by the over-eager application of short
sentences. It was expediency. Overcrowded prisons were undesirable
in themselves and it was expensive to lock people up, the Joint
Under Secretary of State at the Home Office observing in the Debate
that 'it costs £6 11s. a week of the taxpayers' money to keep a man
in prison, and that cost should be avoided if possible' (David
Renton, H.C. Deb. (587) col. 754). (11) The change of attitude in
Parliament is quite striking.

But despite these efforts the problem of overcrowding in the
prisons grew worse. By the middle 1960s it was recognized that the
prison system was seriously overburdened. At the end of 1967, for
example, the population of the general local prisons exceeded their
cellular capacity by about 40 per cent (Sparks, 1971, p.384). A
piece of major legislation was required which would introduce fresh
ideas about the use of alternatives to imprisonment and would permit
the more efficient use of limited resources for those who had to be
confined. The result was a new Criminal Justice Bill.

Parliament was now far less sanguine about the value of prison.
(12) 'The main range of the penal provisions of the Bill', said Mr
Jenkins, the Home Secretary, 'revolves around the single theme, that
of keeping out of prison those who need not be there' (H.C. Deb.
(738) col. 64). The commitment was clear. In opening the Second
Reading Debate, the Home Secretary justified the measures proposed
not by suggesting that they were fairer, more appropriate, or would
have desirable effects on an individual's behaviour, but simply by
asking the question: 'How much effect will all this...have on the
size of the prison population?' (H.C. Deb. (738) col. 69). (13) The

burden on resources was a matter of considerable concern. In fact
the first reason which Mr Jenkins gave for keeping people out of
prison was that
> the overstrain upon prison resources, both of buildings and men,
> is at present appalling. The prison officers are bearing a very
> heavy burden indeed. Without a comparable increase in building
> or staff, the prison population for all establishments has in-
> creased from 11,000 in 1938 to 29,000 in 1964 and to nearly
> 35,000 today.
>
> Such numbers, many of them in for very short periods, make it
> extremely difficult for the essential custodial and rehabilita-
> tive task for men serving sentences of more than a few months to
> be performed. They militate against effective security and also
> against the development of properly organised prison work. (H.C.
> Deb. (738) col. 65)

Lord Stonham painted a more vivid picture in the Lords:
> When half of all sentences are short term, the reception and
> early discharge of large numbers of such prisoners puts an enor-
> mous strain on prison accommodation and staffs. Proper attention
> cannot be given to either security or training. Today we have
> 9,000 men sleeping two or three in a cell designed for one. In
> some prisons overcrowding is such that even sewerage becomes an
> anxiety. In some prisons we have had to increase the jobs which
> can be done sitting down on a chair because there is not enough
> room for anything else. (H.L. Deb. (283) col. 665)

The Home Secretary's second reason for keeping people out of
prison was based on deterrence: 'I want to keep this deterrent
effect a sharp instrument', said Mr Jenkins. 'But by using it too
freely - by getting too many people used to prison too easily - we
blunt our own armoury' (H.C. Deb. (738) col. 65). This suggests
that there was a recognition that although general deterrence might
work, individual deterrence does not.

Two major innovations appeared in the 1967 Act. The suspended
sentence is a clear example of a measure designed to avoid imprisonment if at all possible. The official view had previously opposed
the introduction of suspended sentences: fifteen years earlier the
Advisory Council on the Treatment of Offenders had rejected a proposal that the suspended sentence should be adopted. (14) Its Report
did not mince words:
> The suspended sentence is wrong in principle and to a large
> extent impracticable. It should not be adopted, either in con-
> junction with probation or otherwise. (Home Office, 1957,
> para. 23) (15)

What had occurred in the intervening fifteen years, of course, was
the dramatic rise in the prison population, hence W. F. Deedes'
comment that 'the Home Secretary will be the first to admit that not
least of the pressures behind this clause is the desire to reduce
the number of people who have to be contained in prison' (Standing
Committee A, col. 537).

The other major innovation in the 1967 Act was parole. In contrast with the suspended sentence which may be advocated on the
grounds of individual deterrence, the formal justification for parole is rehabilitative, and it was in language appropriate to the
view of prison as a place of treatment and training that the Government White Paper 'The Adult Offender' was couched. According to the

Government it was
    all the more necessary to seek to overcome (the paradox of train-
    ing men for freedom in conditions of captivity) by strengthening
    links between the prisoner and the free community and by develop-
    ing new ways to ease the transition back to freedom.... (Home
    Office, 1965, para. 1)
The proposal to release people before they need legally be released
was justified with the following:
    Prisoners who do not of necessity have to be detained for the
    protection of the public are in some cases more likely to be made
    into decent citizens if, before completing the whole of their
    sentence, they are released under supervision with a liability to
    recall if they do not behave. (para. 4)
Despite having stated in an earlier paragraph that for many inmates
long periods in prison 'certainly' did not 'fit them for re-entry
into society' (para. 3), the White Paper a few sentences later,
defying all the evidence, reversed course to suggest that rehabilitation in prison was in fact possible. A prisoner's date of release,
it said,
    should be largely dependent upon his response to training and his
    likely behaviour on release. A considerable number of long-term
    prisoners reach a recognisable peak in their training at which
    they may respond to generous treatment, but after which, if kept
    in prison, they may go downhill. To give such prisoners the op-
    portunity of supervised freedom at the right moment may be deci-
    sive in securing their return to decent citizenship. (para. 5)
    (16)
The justifications offered by the White Paper for introducing parole
are particularly interesting:
    These arrangements would afford the strongest incentive to re-
    form, and greatly assist the task of prison administration. It
    would ameliorate the present conditions under which prisoners
    serving long terms of imprisonment become progressively less able
    to re-enter society. It would incidentally also go some way to
    relieve the existing overcrowding in prisons. (para. 8)
How attractive parole appeared because of its potential value in reducing prison overcrowding is a matter of debate. Rupert Cross, for
example, has stated his firm belief that it would be 'quite wrong to
regard prison emptying as the object of this part of the Criminal
Justice Act 1967...' (Cross, 1971, p.97). Nevertheless the suspicion was voiced in Parliament by more than one Member that its purpose was, as S. C. Silkin put it, 'pre-eminently...to reduce the
prison population, and little more than that' (H.C. Deb. (738) col.
176). (17) The Home Secretary had described parole when introducing the Second Reading Debate as 'a matter affecting the prison
population of medium and long-term prisoners' (H.C. Deb. (738) col.
69), and having outlined the proposed system went on to say that
'(al)together, the reduction in the average daily prison population
might be about 600' (H.C. Deb. (738) col. 70). In addition to the
reduction in numbers, Parliament was also reminded of the economic
advantages of parole: 'if we adopt the system whereby men are released from prison on licence', it was said, 'the overall cost must
be reduced. It is very expensive to keep a prisoner in a close
(sic) or other prison...' (Mr Victor Yates, H.C. Deb. (738) col.
131). (18) The medium and long-term prisoners to whom the Home

Secretary had referred are, of course, the most expensive to keep in custody.

The parole provisions provoked more debate in Parliament than any other section of the Criminal Justice Bill. Even so, there was no disagreement about the desirability of introducing a parole system: the only real point of contention was about the authority which was to select prisoners. (19)

Though parole is generally accepted as a success, the suspended sentence has proved more controversial. The population levels in English prisons did at first decline. But the decline was short-lived. Within two years, the number of prisoners had surpassed its former level. By 1970 there were about 40,000 in prison service establishments, compared with the 30,000 of five years before (Sparks, 1971, p.385). Study of the suspended sentence revealed that with its introduction there had been, as some Members of Parliament had feared, a reduction in the numbers of those fined or put on probation. The view in the Home Office was that only between 40 and 60 per cent of those given suspended sentences would have received sentences of immediate imprisonment before 1968 (20) (H.C. Deb. (826) col. 188), and an analysis by Richard Sparks has estimated that a quarter of all those given suspended sentences in 1969 would have been fined before the 1967 Act came into force (1971, p.387). The courts were therefore sometimes making orders suspending sentence (which they sometimes had subsequently to activate) when they would previously have imposed fines or probation: (21) in other words the courts were extending the potential application of imprisonment to a wider range of offenders, thus ensuring that what had been meant to be used as an alternative to imprisonment was in some cases being used as an alternative to other non-custodial methods. Perhaps the deterrent nature of the suspended sentence also exacerbates the problem. If a suspended sentence is to be taken seriously as a threat, it is possible that the courts may feel it necessary to impose a longer suspended term than they would if they were handing down a sentence of immediate imprisonment. Furthermore, a court which has to decide whether or not to activate a suspended sentence may feel constrained to order that it take effect so as to demonstrate that a suspended sentence is intended to be taken seriously. (22) It was said in the Commons to be impossible to calculate the effect of the suspended sentence on the length of prison terms served (H.C. Deb. (826) col. 188), (23) though the view was put forward that the evidence suggested that the suspended sentence had increased their duration (H.C. Deb. (826) col. 998). Richard Sparks has little doubt about this:

> It would not be surprising if implemented suspended sentences had doubled the effective lengths (of terms)...of offenders imprisoned after having been given a suspended sentence. The effect of this, in turn, could well be to increase the prison population by as much as 25-30 per cent.... (1971, p.393) (24)

Legislation again failed, however, to make any favourable impact on the overcrowding problem. Indeed the situation soon deteriorated, prompting further efforts from Parliament. When Mr Maudling, now the Home Secretary, opened the Debate on the 1972 Criminal Justice Bill, he did not acknowledge the failure of the suspended sentence but said that it was largely as a concomitant of the increase in

offences of violence that there had been an enormous increase in the
prison population (which was then about four times the size it was
before the war). 'This leads', he went on, 'to very grave overcrowding in our prisons' (H.C. Deb. (826) col. 966). It would seem from
these Debates that the more acute administrative difficulties become,
the more readily their importance is recognized. The customary justifications citing rehabilitation as a reason for introducing or
modifying penal measures now took second place to administrative
considerations.

The conditions in our prisons...are very serious. We must pay
   particular attention to this problem of overcrowding, which in
   itself is bad but is also important in that it makes the job of
   the prison service much more difficult and the possibility of
   rehabilitation and redemption far less likely than it otherwise
   would be. (Mr Maudling, H.C. Deb. (826) col. 966)

The 1972 Criminal Justice Act continues the attempt to make the
penal system more flexible by providing the courts with further innovations in the search for more appropriate penalties. The basic
assumption was that it was due to the lack of alternatives that the
courts had continued to use imprisonment, (25) an assumption shared
by the Advisory Council on the Penal System in its 'Report on Non-
custodial and Semi-custodial Penalties', published in 1970, in which
it referred to the 'widely held view amongst sentencers that many
offenders are sentenced to imprisonment, not because this is in itself the sentence of choice, but, in effect, for lack of any more
appropriate alternative' (para. 8). The Debates on the 1972 Bill
suggest that Parliament has established a presumption that all adult
offenders should now be dealt with by a non-custodial measure unless
they fall into a small, clearly-defined group. (26) The Home Secretary presumably attempted to define this irreducible minimum when he
argued that 'those who need not be sent to prison, those who are not
guilty of violent crimes, should be punished in other ways in the
interests of relieving the strain on the prison service and in the
interests of the community' (H.C. Deb. (826) col. 972).

Again, the pressure did not only come from the need to reduce the
numbers confined. The economic motive was referred to in even more
explicit fashion: it was said by Edmund Dell MP to be 'not in issue
that even from the point of view of the Chancellor of the Exchequer
the Government will be making a good investment, because...each
person kept out of prison represents a saving of £24 a week' (H.C.
Deb. (837) col. 1782). (27)

With its emphasis on community service, compensation and restitution, and day training centres, the 1972 Act suggests another shift
in the justifications for English penal policy. Now the formal commitment seems to be turning towards reintegrating offenders with the
use of non-custodial measures. This may serve several purposes. It
might help inculcate a sense of social responsibility and it might
involve the community in the treatment of offenders. It might show
the public that taxpayers' money is being well spent and it might
demonstrate that delinquents have a contribution to make. Perhaps
this is all a consequence of the current view that criminal behaviour is not 'abnormal' behaviour. But though the justifications
may change, the underlying pressures remain the same.

Prisons in England are still seriously overcrowded. There is a certain irony in the present situation. Efforts have been made to develop a number of alternatives to imprisonment, yet the prison population remains swollen. The courts are aware of the criticisms levelled against imprisonment, yet they have been making greater use of longer terms. Though many cherish their hopes, some are now not only sceptical about the value of imprisonment, but about alternatives to imprisonment as well. Indeed, a greater emphasis on non-custodial alternatives is not without its own problems.

First, what is the rationale for the use of non-custodial measures, on what grounds do we justify their use? Some would argue in correctional terms, suggesting that such methods are more successful in encouraging offenders not to break the law in future. It is generally assumed (without much evidence) that the fine is quite successful in deterring subsequent law-breaking, (28) but there is little to suggest that other forms of non-custodial treatment produce 'better' results than imprisonment. We are on firmer ground if we simply acknowledge that it is more humane and less costly to employ non-custodial methods whenever possible. What non-custodial methods purport to accomplish, of course, is not only of great importance to the courts when they have to make sentencing decisions but also is often intended to contribute to the public understanding of the penal system. Some commentators believe that there is a risk that non-custodial measures - especially the more recent additions to the penal system - may be employed by the courts indiscriminately, through ignorance, misunderstanding or over-enthusiasm (Prins, 1973). Alternatives to imprisonment, as a result, may not be used as they were intended to be used and this may lead either to their being considered ineffective, or even (as seems to have happened with the suspended sentence) to their accomplishing precisely the opposite of what was intended. Parliament has attempted to make available to the courts a more flexible penal system which offers a wider range of more appropriate methods of disposal. But in the absence of any clear knowledge of what non-custodial measures may actually be able to achieve, it is quite possible that the courts will be confused by the range of available measures. If the courts become confused then offenders and the public certainly will. Confusion will do nothing to minimize disparities in sentence. While there is no satisfactory evidence about the outcome of non-custodial measures, the courts will have to make assumptions about the effectiveness and significance of various measures if they wish to meet offenders' 'needs'; this is in itself more likely to encourage them to rely on a less utilitarian approach in sentencing and to resort to the notion of 'deserts'.

Second, problems are likely to arise as a result of the complex nature of the sentencing decision and the need of the courts to meet aims other than the rehabilitation of reintegration of offenders. Courts have to resolve the tension which exists between custodial and non-custodial penalties, yet there is often little consensus as to what should be done with offenders. Imprisonment serves a variety of social functions; the courts, for example, are well aware of the sentiments of a substantial proportion of the public on the

treatment of offenders and its need to be reassured that wrong-doers
are being incapacitated and punished. In certain kinds of case the
courts will consequently be strongly tempted to use the sanction of
imprisonment, however many non-custodial penalties are provided,
simply because prison symbolizes the worse that society can do as a
formal punishment to someone guilty of a grave crime or someone continually in serious trouble. Courts are still heavily influenced in
making the sentencing decision by the criminal act and prior record
of the offender. The appropriateness of punishment, it seems, still
tends to be defined largely on the basis of the offender's deserts
rather than his needs. In other cases the courts wish by imposing a
severe sentence not only to express the disapproval of the community
for the criminal behaviour but also to deter potential offenders.
(29) Non-custodial alternatives, in contrast, suggest considerable
leniency in the treatment of offenders, simply because they do not
involve deprivation of liberty. Courts are unlikely to find non-
custodial measures appropriate in these circumstances either to sym-
bolize disapproval or to deter others since it has long been assumed
that the punishment of imprisonment resides in its deprivation of
liberty. Besides, prison has to remain the final sanction if non-
custodial methods fail. The result will be an irreducible minimum
of offenders who will continue to be sent to prison. New alternatives, such as those introduced by the 1972 Criminal Justice Act,
are more likely to be used by the courts as alternatives to other
more traditional forms of non-custodial treatment, and perhaps to
the detriment of both. One answer might be to give the courts non-
custodial or semi-custodial measures involving greater control of
offenders which will appear less to them, offenders and general
public as leniency, though this will tax the imagination. (30)
Another problem stemming from the connotations of leniency inevitably borne by non-custodial measures is the risk that if an offender undergoing a non-custodial method of treatment is brought before
the court charged with a further offence, the court may wish to sym-
bolize its disapproval of the failure to grasp a generous opportunity previously given. This may lead to an inclination not only to
impose a prison sentence, but a prison sentence longer than that
which might otherwise be considered appropriate. 'The search for
solutions is not a simple one', Empey has written of the situation
in America. 'We tend to operate in extremes. If the minimal con-
trols of the suspended sentence or probation do not work, we tend
either to incarcerate or to plan elaborate therapeutic treatment.
Neither extreme may be warranted for the majority of cases' (1967,
p.50). From the viewpoint of those who administer the penal system
there is also a certain amount of risk in extending non-custodial
measures. If an offender being dealt with in the community commits
an offence, he - and the penal system - may attract adverse publicity. This may be especially true of men released on parole and
those taking part in hostel schemes. Hostile publicity undermines
public confidence in the penal system and the competence of its administrators. It may bring about changes in practice which are
undesirable from the point of view of penal policy (however much
they may appear to add to public safety) (Hawkins, 1971, pp.187-92,
208-11). At the same time it may encourage probation officers and
others who work with offenders to lay greater emphasis upon security

and control, at the expense of whatever else they may be trying to
achieve.

Third, to concentrate upon the use of non-custodial measures may
also cause manpower problems. It is customary to impose on the Probation and After-Care service for the personnel to implement new
penal measures. It is a familiar fact that there are never enough
probation officers, never enough people of the right temperament and
training contemplating a career in the service. It is an equally
familiar fact that probation officers are grossly underpaid. While
the search goes on for a more flexible penal system and at the same
time the probation service is expected to do more and more, we place
a wider set of demands upon probation officers' expertise and versatility. Following the 1972 Act, for example, officers will have to
adapt to working with groups and with volunteers.

Finally, the eagerness with which the search for new methods of
dealing with offenders in the community is pursued may lead to an
indifference towards or even neglect of imprisonment and the very
problems which prompted the search in the first place. People are
now being sent to prison for longer periods. At the same time,
greater efforts are being made to keep less serious offenders out of
prison entirely and to release the better risks from prison early.
The change of policy produces a residue of potentially tougher and
more difficult prisoners. The response of prison regimes is likely
to be a greater consciousness of security and control. Prison officials in California, for example, customarily lay part of the blame
for the bitter discontent in their state prisons on the introduction
of the Probation Subsidy Program.

V

Perhaps there are two lessons in particular to be learned from all
of this. The more important is that it is not wise to initiate further schemes first without explicit objectives being set for them;
second, without some reliable evidence on which to judge whether
those objectives are capable of being fulfilled; and third without
much more substantial monitoring of their effectiveness.

The other lesson, whether we like it or not, is that we have to
learn to live with imprisonment for the foreseeable future. Norval
Morris has confidently predicted that 'before the end of this century, prison...will become extinct, though the word may live on to
cover quite different social organizations' (1965, p.268). This is
an unconventional opinion. The conclusions of Cohen and Taylor in
their study of the experience of long-term imprisonment are surely
nearer the mark:

we see no evidence for the emergence of any alternative policy to
the containment of an increasing number of criminals in conditions like those we have described. (1972, p.187)

The official view is the same:

no large modern state has found it possible to dispense with some
form of imprisonment. Whatever may be the changes in our penal
system in the last third of the twentieth century there is no immediate prospect of the prison system withering away. Indeed it
is likely that there will be more people in custody in the next

few years than ever before. (Home Office, 1969, para. 245)
If this is the case, one of the major needs is to assist the courts
in attaining the irreducible minimum (assuming they have not already
done so). To do this demands greater consistency in sentencing as
well as the provision of a body of knowledge about sentencing outcomes which may help guide the courts' discretion, so that they do
not send people to prison when they do not know what else to do with
them. Though it would be a complex, difficult and possibly dis-
tasteful task, Parliament could give the courts a useful impetus to
encourage greater use of non-custodial alternatives by providing a
clear and detailed set of sentencing aims and criteria. This clari-
fication could obviously be reviewed periodically in the light of
changing social and economic conditions. Meanwhile the courts could
make a significant contribution in reducing the burden on the prisons by trying to achieve an all-round reduction in sentencing tar-
iffs. (31) To provide further alternatives to imprisonment in an
effort to make the penal system yet more flexible is to risk clut-
tering it up with methods which will merely detract from traditional
alternatives like probation. It might even be better to revitalize
the existing system by administering it in a more humane, efficient
and imaginative manner, rather than to spend time, energy and resources in casting about for further alternatives.

NOTES

1 I do not propose to deal with unsentenced prisoners, though there
has been a similar concern to restrict the use of imprisonment for
this group. Though I shall use the terms 'non-custodial measures'
and 'alternatives to imprisonment' interchangeably they are not, of
course, the same thing. The two terms illustrate the different
methods employed for the treatment of young and adult offenders.
Youthful delinquents excite more sympathy and understanding than
adult criminals and we are more willing to use methods which we hope
will educate, guide or support. Though such methods usually involve
custody, they are not intended (with the exception of the detention
centre) to be punitive. They are, however, intended to serve as
alternatives to imprisonment. The development of the penal system
for adults has been characterized by the adoption of methods which
rely less on paternalistic conceptions of residential training and
education. The shift here, paradoxically, has been towards non-
custodial measures, such as fines, suspended sentence, or community
service.
2 This question is dealt with by Roger Hood (1974).
3 The detention centre is an exception to the general pattern since
it was originally intended to act as an individual deterrent to
youthful offenders by making life unpleasant for them for a time.
But detention centre regimes have also grown less harsh.
4 For example, one of the aims of the Special Intensive Parole Unit
studies which were carried out in California some years ago was to
see what effect early release from prison with more intensive parole
supervision had upon the behaviour of the individuals involved. In
fact, the parole revocation rates showed in general that the experimental intensive supervision seemed to produce no more successful

results than the conventional practice. However the experiments
were still justified as valuable because it was realized that although there was little change in terms of behavioural outcome, the
shorter periods of imprisonment called for as part of the experimental treatment resulted in significant financial savings to the State
of California.

5   In 'The End of Ideology' Daniel Bell observes that social control agencies can exert the necessary political pressures in order
to maintain or increase funds. One agency released a 'reckless' and
inflationary statistic because it hoped 'by shocking the public, to
mobilize pressure for an increased appropriation at the next session
of the legislature. Such "inflation" of crime is a not uncommon
feature of law enforcement in the United States today' (1962, pp.157-
8).

6   The search for alternatives to imprisonment has of course been
going on for more than the last thirty years: the Probation of Offenders Act 1907, the Children Act and the Prevention of Crime Act
(both of 1908), the Mental Deficiency Act 1913, and the Criminal
Justice Act 1914 all attempted to remove certain kinds of offenders
from prison and provide more suitable alternatives. Indeed the
latter has been described by Rupert Cross as 'the most effective
prison emptier that has ever got onto the Statute Book' (p.21).

7   In similar vein Lord Jowitt, the Lord Chancellor, thought imprisonment of young offenders was the 'greatest mistake we can make
...unless it is absolutely necessary...' (H.L. Deb. (155) cols
391-2).

8   In forming its opinion the court was obliged to consider information about the offender and give reasons if it thought no other
method was appropriate (s. 17(2), (3)).

9   This thinking also led to the introduction of two entirely new
penal methods for young offenders: detention centres and attendance
centres. The former show the Act to be opposed to imprisonment for
these offenders, but not to confinement.

10   The First Offenders Act 1958 was followed by the Criminal Justice Act 1961. The focus of this statute was not on adult offenders. It took the approach of the 1948 Act a little further, again
limiting the application of imprisonment by preventing the imposi-
tion of terms of medium length on those under twenty one (s. 3(1)).
Familiar arguments were heard in the Debates on this legislation,
though one Member did refer to the desirability of protecting the
young offender from the stigma of imprisonment (a view in direct
contrast with that of Sir Samuel Hoare in the 1938 Debates) (Mr Alan
Brown, H.C. Deb. (630) col. 659).

11   Not all Members, however, were willing to lay such emphasis upon
expediency as a reason for modifying penal practice. One, for example, confessed to 'grave misgivings' about the Bill because of 'an
ugly suspicion that (it was) a case of manipulating justice to meet
expediency.' 'Great play', he continued, 'has been made of the
overcrowding of our prisons' (S. L. C. Maydon, H.C. Deb. (587) col.
742). Another referred to the 'materialistic' reasons of the Home
Office in wishing to reduce the prison population. There would be
'fewer prisons to build, fewer prisons to reconstruct, fewer warders
to provide, fewer prison visitors to escort, less clothing, less
food and less cost generally' (Sir Thomas Moore, H.C. Deb. (587)
col. 740).

12   Its attitude is perhaps best summed up in the elegant and con-
cise comments of the late Sidney Silverman made when he was debating
the proposed abolition of Penal Servitude and Corrective Training:
    They are abandoned now. They are abandoned because they were
    harsh, unjust, oppressive and totally ineffective. They were
    based on the notion that punishment, particularly by imprison-
    ment, was a valuable thing in itself. We all know that that is
    not true, and we all know that no man ever came out of prison
    after a prison sentence a better man than he was before he went
    in. (H.C. Deb. (738) col. 121)
13   And in the Lords, a former Conservative Home Secretary, Lord
Brooke of Cumnor, expressed the view that knowing how seriously
overcrowded the prisons are is 'in itself a reason for seeking to
avoid unnecessary prison sentences of all kinds' (H.L. Deb. (283)
col. 652).
14   Though it was published in 1957 as Appendix D to the Advisory
Council's Report on 'Alternatives to Short Terms of Imprisonment',
the Report on the suspended sentence had in fact been presented in
1952.
15   Under s. 39 of the Criminal Justice Act 1967 a court which
passed a sentence of not more than two years' imprisonment could
make an order suspending sentence. To emphasize the need to keep
people out of prison a provision was added which compelled the court
to suspend sentence where the sentence was for a term of not more
than six months and the offender had had no prior experience of
prison or borstal (s. 39(3)), with the exception of certain serious
cases involving violence, firearms or explosives (s. 39(3)(a)).
Suspension of sentence was not mandatory in certain other circumstances: see s. 39(3)(b)(c)(d). If an offence was committed by a
person already under suspended sentence, the court need not order
that the suspended sentence take effect, if it found that it would
be unjust to do so in the circumstances (s. 40(1)). In this case
it could either take no action, or extend the period of the original
order, or order that the sentence take effect but for a shorter
period than that originally prescribed (s. 40(1)).
16   For further critical comments about the so-called 'peak' response to prison training see Hood (1973).
17   See also, for example, the comments in Standing Committee A of
T. L. Iremonger at col. 724.
18   The economic argument had been used before in the Debates on the
1961 Criminal Justice Bill; see the comments by T. L. Iremonger MP
at H.C. Deb. (630) col. 652.
19   Under the system which was adopted in the 1967 Act, prisoners
serving medium or long sentences are eligible to have quite substantial reductions made in their terms if selected for parole. An
inmate is eligible after serving not less than one-third of his sentence or twelve months (whichever is longer) (s. 60(1)). On release parolees are supervised in the community by members of the
Probation and After-Care Service. If the parolee fails to abide by
the conditions of his release he may have his licence revoked and be
returned to prison. The power to revoke has been sparingly used:
so far only about 6 or 8 per cent of parolees are returned to prison
each year. Fears that the introduction of parole would provoke
some courts into raising the levels of their sentences in an effort

to prevent the paroling authorities from releasing prisoners too
soon (thereby adding to the burden on the prisons), do not seem to
have been realized.
20 Mark Carlisle MP, in a written answer to Edmund Dell MP.
21 Lord Parker CJ had found 'many instances' where courts had not
known what sentence to impose and had given suspended sentences,
where probation was the proper order: R v O'Keefe (1969) All ER 426
at 427.
22 See also the remarks of Edward Lyons MP in H.C. Deb. (826) cols
1003-10.
23 Written answer of Mark Carlisle MP to Edmund Dell MP.
24 Sparks has also suggested that the suspended sentence was more
likely to affect those sent to open prisons, in which overcrowding
is not permitted to occur (p.394). Leon Radzinowicz (1971) has
argued that the suspended sentence has tended to emerge in more
rigid legal systems; thus it may be a progressive measure in countries with very few alternatives to prison, but retrogressive when
applied in a country like Britain which possesses a highly-developed
probation system. Not all commentators have been gloomy in their
assessments of the suspended sentence. Ella Oatham and Frances
Simon have concluded that its introduction was responsible for a cut
in the prison population of between 850 and 1,900, though they also
suggest that another effect has been to increase the average length
of sentence (p.235).
25 See the comments of Sir David Renton, H.C. Deb. (826) col. 991.
26 Thus the formula employed in the 1948 and 1958 Acts which res-
tricts courts from imposing imprisonment unless 'of opinion that no
other method...is appropriate' is extended in s. 14(1) of the 1972
Act to apply to 'a person who has attained the age of twenty-one and
has not previously been sentenced to imprisonment....'
27 The Act modified the provisions for suspended sentence, the most
significant replacing the requirement for mandatory suspension in
certain cases with a discretionary power (s. 11(1)). It also made
provision for the possibility of an order to attend a day training
centre to be added as a condition of probation (s. 20). More significant perhaps is the new form of non-custodial penalty made
available to the courts by the Act. It is intended that the community service order will be seen by the courts and the public as a
viable alternative to the shorter custodial sentence (Home Office,
1972, para. 32). The intent of this penalty is as much a deprivation of leisure as of liberty (though there is a rather doubtful
assumption here about offenders' modes of work and leisure). A
further innovation was the power given to the courts by s. 22 to
defer passing sentence on an offender after conviction for a specific period up to six months. The aim of this section is to enable
courts to select the most appropriate sentence by making it possible to take into account the offender's conduct after some expected change in his circumstances. In s. 37 there is a further guard
against the unnecessary use of imprisonment in the provision that
no-one shall be sentenced for the first time to a custodial sentence
(that is, including suspended sentence, borstal and detention
centre) unless legally represented.
28 But this assumption is now under attack: see Bottoms (1973).
29 General deterrence receives powerful support as a major aim of

sentencing; for example the Police Federation of England and Wales
in evidence to the Royal Commission on the Penal System said:
Whilst we welcome the more humane approach to the problem of
crime and accept the importance of rehabilitating the criminal,
we would not wish to see any policy of penal reform which did not
clearly recognise the deterrent theory as the main objective of
punishment. (Home Office, 1967, vol. III, part 2, p.6)
30 Rupert Cross, for instance, has suggested the use of a highly
intensive form of probation supervision (1971, p.169).
31 Dutch courts appear to have made substantial progress in this
respect: see D. Cohen (1972).

REFERENCES

BELL, D. (1962), 'The End of Ideology', New York: Free Press.
BOTTOMS, A.E. (1973), The Efficacy of the Fine: the Case for
Agnosticism, 'Criminal Law Review', pp.543-51.
COHEN, D. (1972), Out of Jail, 'New Society', 4 May, vol.20, no.501,
pp.234-5.
COHEN, S. and TAYLOR, L. (1972), 'Psychological Survival: the Ex-
perience of Long-Term Imprisonment', Harmondsworth: Penguin Books.
CONRAD, J. (1965), 'Crime and its Correction', Berkeley: University
of California Press.
CROSS, A.R.N. (1971), 'Punishment, Prison and the Public', Stevens.
EMPEY, L.T. (1967), 'Alternatives to Incarceration', Washington, DC:
HEW.
HALL WILLIAMS, J.E. (1970), 'The English Penal System in Transition',
Butterworths.
HAWKINS, K.O. (1971), 'Parole Selection: the American Experience',
unpublished PhD dissertation, Cambridge University.
HOME OFFICE (1957), Advisory Council on the Treatment of Offenders,
'Alternatives to Short Terms of Imprisonment', HMSO.
HOME OFFICE (1965), 'The Adult Offender', HMSO: Cmnd 2852.
HOME OFFICE (1967), Royal Commission on the Penal System, 'Written
Evidence from Government Departments, Miscellaneous Bodies and Indi-
vidual Witnesses', HMSO.
HOME OFFICE (1969), 'People in Prison (England and Wales)', HMSO:
Cmnd 4214.
HOME OFFICE (1970), Advisory Council on the Penal System, 'Non-
custodial and Semi-custodial Penalties', HMSO.
HOME OFFICE (1972), 'The Criminal Justice Act 1972. A Guide for the
Courts', HMSO.
HOOD, R.G. (1973), 'Some Fundamental Dilemmas of the English Parole
System and a Suggestion for an Alternative Structure', paper given
at Cropwood Round-table Conference on Parole, Cambridge.
HOOD, R.G. (1974), Criminology and Penal Change: a Case Study of
the Nature and Impact of some Recent Advice to Government, in 'Crime,
Criminology and Public Policy, Heinemann.
McCLEAN, J.D. and WOOD, J.C. (1969), 'Criminal Justice and the
Treatment of Offenders', Sweet & Maxwell.
MANNHEIM, H. (1939), 'The Dilemma of Penal Reform', Allen & Unwin.
MORRIS, N. (1965), Prison in Evolution, in T. Grygier, H. Jones and
J.C. Spencer (eds), 'Criminology in Transition', Tavistock.

OATHAM, E. and SIMON, F. (1972), Are Suspended Sentences Working?,
'New Society', 3 August, vol.21, no.514, pp.233-5.
PRINS, H.A. (1973), 'Non-custodial Measures: Trends and Develop-
ments', unpublished paper given at Fifth National Conference on
Teaching and Research in Criminology, Cambridge, 4-6 July.
RADZINOWICZ, L. (1971), A Foreseeable Failure, 'Sunday Times', 24
January.
ROSE, G. (1961), 'The Struggle for Penal Reform', Stevens.
SMITH, R.L. (1967), Probation Subsidy: Success Story, 'Youth Autho-
rity Quarterly', Winter, pp.11-16.
SMITH, R.L. (1968), 1969 - A Year of Decision, 'Youth Authority
Quarterly', vol.21, no.4, pp.3-6.
SPARKS, R.F. (1971), The Use of Suspended Sentences, 'Criminal Law
Review', pp.384-401.
WALKER, N.D. (1968), 'Crime and Punishment in Britain', Edinburgh
University Press, 2nd ed.
WEBB, S. and B. (1922), 'English Prisons under Local Government',
Longmans.

Probation of Offenders Act 1907.
Children Act 1908.
Prevention of Crime Act 1908.
Mental Deficiency Act 1913.
Criminal Justice Act 1914.
Criminal Justice Act 1948.
First Offenders Act 1958.
Criminal Justice Act 1961.
Criminal Justice Act 1967.
Criminal Justice Act 1972.
Hansard, House of Commons Debates.
Hansard, House of Lords Debates.
R. v. O'Keefe (1969) 1 All E.R. 426.

Other sources

CHESTER, L. (1971), Prisons: the Reform that went Wrong, 'Sunday
Times', 24 January.
CRIMINAL LAW REVIEW (1973), pp.3-35, Symposium on the Criminal Jus-
tice Act 1972, including:
    McLean, I., Compensation and Restitution Orders, pp.3-6.
    White, S., Suspended Imprisonment, pp.7-11.
    Blom-Cooper, L., Postponing Sentence, pp.12-15.
    Wootton, B., Community Service, pp.16-20.
    Bottoms, A.E., Day Training Centres, pp.21-3.
JEPSON, N.A. (1972), The Value of Prison?, 'Howard Journal', vol.13,
no.3, pp.234-45.
RADICAL ALTERNATIVES TO PRISON (1970), 'The Case for Radical Alter-
natives to Prison', Christian Action Publications.
SAMUELS, A. (1971), Penal Reform: How to Reduce the Prison Popula-
tion, 'Contemporary Review', vol.219, no.1266, pp.19-25.
SPARKS, R.F. (1971), 'Local Prisons; the Crisis in the English
Penal System', Heinemann.

I am grateful to Roger Hood and Donald Harris for their helpful criticisms of an earlier draft of this paper, which was written before publication of the Report of the Advisory Council on the Penal System on 'Young Adult Offenders'.

Chapter 7

TACTICS OF REFORM

Martin Wright

Time and again in our history significant social reforms have
depended on a co-ordinated lead from a small minority, but the
balance of necessary impetus may now be changing as traditional
assumptions about the pattern of authority and society break down.
There has to be substantial popular interest and support for the
aims of an enlightened penal policy and for the methods we use to
carry it out. Rt Hon. Roy Jenkins, Home Secretary, 1974.

One of the most depressing aspects of history is human ingenuity in
devising punishments, readiness to use them, and inability to distinguish their actual from their intended effects. But there have
also been some who resisted the prevailing view: sometimes at the
grass-roots, as when juries refused to convict because, they thought
the death penalty for larceny too severe; more often a small group
of specialist reformers.

This chapter is mainly about tactics. An outline of the development of the penal reform movement will show the range of techniques
used by reformers over the years, and still today, as with small
resources they apply pressure and persuasion to the Home Office,
Parliament and the public. After a section on the combination of
old and new methods employed in the early 1970s, there will be some
suggestions as to the directions in which future progress may be
made.

The chief pioneer of penal reform was John Howard, whose concern
developed on a pattern which has been followed by many other reformers. He became aware of the problem, almost by chance, when in
1773 he was appointed Sheriff of Bedfordshire and one of his duties
was to inspect Bedford gaol. He collected facts - being horrified
by the degradation he had seen, he wanted to know if other prisons
were as bad. He published his findings - 'The State of the Prisons'
appeared in four editions from 1777 to 1790, and the weight of
amassed detail about the institutions he visited, in England and
later abroad, condemned prevailing conditions more tellingly than
any amount of emotional prose. Finally, he put them before parlia-
mentarians and other influential people, with the help of his
friend Samuel Whitbread MP, to try to induce action.

Other individual reformers followed. Sir Samuel Romilly campaigned in parliament against the death penalty for property

offences. Alexander Maconochie tried to reform the system from
within, by means of a demonstration project. As governor of the remote penal colony of Norfolk Island, 800 miles from Australia, with
a mixed population of singly and doubly convicted men, he attempted
to encourage rather than punish them: in his system convicts were
awarded marks for good conduct, by which they could earn early release. Surprisingly few were reconvicted. But Maconochie had
flouted the punitive ideology of his day; being several months'
travelling time from London he was not in a position to lobby, and
was brusquely removed. The story of his achievement, and the unhappy end to his career, is well told by Barry (1958). In 1866 the
Howard Association was formed to campaign against such prison bar-
barities as the crank and the treadmill, and against capital punishment. It advocated probation, from 1881 onwards, parole (1904) and
restitution to the victim (1906); in 1872 it took a prominent part
in the London international penitentiary congress (Rose, 1961). The
Association, however, lost momentum and influence towards the end of
the century, partly because official policies were apparently suc-
ceeding in bringing down the prison population, but partly also because of the refusal of its secretary, William Tallack, to accept
the growing weight of evidence and opinion against his particular
remedy, the 'separate system' of imprisonment. The next major initiative was achieved largely by a press campaign instigated by a
prison chaplain, the Rev. W.D. Morrison. This led to the setting up
of the Gladstone Committee whose Report (1895) was followed by several worthwhile reforms.
      Penal reform received a new impetus in the 1920s. In 1921
Margery Fry founded the Howard League for Penal Reform by merging
the Penal Reform League and the Howard Association, and became its
first secretary; she remained actively involved all her life as
successively chairman, vice-chairman and committee member. In the
same year Maurice Waller took over the chairmanship of the Prison
Commission, and in 1922 Alexander Paterson became a commissioner;
her friendship with these two reform-minded prison chiefs helped to
achieve many improvements, such as abolition of the convicts' hair
crop, the broad arrow on prison clothing, and the silence rule, and
the reintroduction of prison visitors to provide some slight unofficial contact with the outside world.
      Margery Fry was succeeded by Cicely Craven, who had a very dif-
ferent style: direct attack and open criticism of government policies. Those who knew her say that she was at her best when facing a
critical audience (Klare, 1974). A magistrate, like Miss Fry, she
was much concerned with improvements in court procedure, the treatment of children and raising the age of criminal responsibility.
Much of her work was through parliament: the Howard League drafted
and promoted the Poor Prisoners' Defence Act 1930 and the Summary
Jurisdiction (Appeals) Act 1933, and helped to secure the passing
of the Money Payments (Justices' Procedure) Act 1935. The League
led the campaign which secured the setting up of the Departmental
Committee on Corporal Punishment under Sir Edward Cadogan, whose
Report (1938) firmly recommended the abolition of corporal punishment as a penal sanction, on the basis of both moral considerations
and research results. In 1938 a Bill incorporating this and other
reforms was presented by the Home Secretary, Sir Samuel Hoare (later

Lord Templewood); but its passage was prevented by the 1939-45
war and it finally emerged as the Criminal Justice Act 1948. Several of those who took a prominent part in promoting its passage
through Parliament were, or later became, leading members of the
Howard League, which had, through its Parliamentary Penal Reform
Group, proposed several amendments to the Bill.

Another method of bringing about reform is the demonstration project, and the Howard League experimented with two of these. In 1930
it raised the money for the introduction of an experimental prisoners' earnings scheme (this was strictly speaking a re-introduc-
tion: prisoners were able to earn money by their work in the early
nineteenth century); unfortunately no one has subsequently succeeded in increasing the amount above pocket-money level. In 1944-5
it introduced wireless and correspondence courses for prisoners,
thus gaining a foothold for education which was consolidated in 1967
by the appointment of an educationalist as Chief Education Officer,
and in 1972 by the Criminal Justice Act which, by establishing Day
Training Centres, recognized that if an offender needed education
(in the widest sense) to help him to earn a law-abiding living, this
could take place outside prison.

With Hugh Klare's period as secretary, from 1950 to 1971, the
Howard League moved from being an organization run largely by voluntary workers to one primarily employing paid staff. He believed
(Klare, 1974) that 'the general public was unsympathetic to penal
reform and that progress could best be achieved through discussions
with enlightened decision-makers like Sir Lionel Fox and R.A. Butler.'   Butler was Conservative Home Secretary from 1955 to 1961;
Fox regarded the Howard League as 'H.M. Opposition to the Prison
Commission', of which he was chairman from 1942 to 1960 (Rose,
1961, p.280). But although it never hesitated to use its contacts,
the League never compromised its financial independence by seeking
a government grant: as the Annual Report for 1950-1 observes, if it
were not wholly independent, it would be neither free to criticize
and bring pressure to bear, nor even to educate public opinion
except along lines acceptable to the authorities. Nor did it rely
exclusively on polite persuasion. It circulated a questionnaire to
ex-prisoners which Mark Benney used for his book 'Gaol Delivery'
(1948), documenting once again the squalid futility of the prison
regime.

It also continued its parliamentary activity: in 1958 two Acts
aimed at restricting the use of imprisonment were passed, both originally proposed by the Howard League. The First Offenders' Act,
introduced as a private member's bill by Sir George Benson, required magistrates to give written reasons before sending a first
offender to prison; the Maintenance Orders Act allowed courts to
order the deduction from wages of the amounts owing on maintenance
or affiliation orders. In addition, the League formed a new parliamentary penal reform group in 1960, and urged amendments in the
Criminal Justice Acts of 1961, 1967 and, working closely with
NACRO, in 1972.

Many other ideas proposed or supported by the Howard League were
eventually adopted; they include the abolition of the detention
centre for girls, the provision of probation homes and hostels, and
the training of magistrates and withholding from them the power to

commit to borstal. Inevitably, many others still have not been
accepted, or have been introduced only partially: for example censorship of prisoners' correspondence has been limited only slightly,
few new prisons have yet been built in such a way as to avoid slop-
ping out, a practice which has aroused the impotent disgust of reformers at least since Paterson (Playfair, 1971, p.109), guard dogs
have been introduced despite the League's objections, and there has
been no substantial increase in pay since the original demonstration
project. These and many others remain, regrettably, on the agenda.
    Klare's idea of the penal reformer became increasingly that of a
specialist, aiming to improve prison conditions by organic or struc-
tural methods: by understanding interpersonal relations in penal
institutions, so as to give the staff a more positive role and thus
reduce negative pressures. Prison conditions can be much improved
in this way, as has been shown by the relatively slight prison subculture achieved at Grendon: this psychiatric prison, originally
proposed by two Prison Commission medical officers, Drs Norwood East
and W.H. Hubert, was established in 1960, after pressure by the
Howard League in support of the scheme's advocates within the Home
Office. Like his chairman Benson, Klare also saw the importance of
facts in aiding reform: not merely the compilation of observations
in the tradition of Howard, Hobhouse and Brockway (1922), and Benney
(1948), valuable though these always are, but scientific research.
Thus the Annual Report for 1950-1 records that £1,500 had, for the
first time, been included in the Civil Estimates for research by the
Home Office; 'the inclusion is largely due to the efforts of your
Committee'. The League also proposed in 1956-7 the creation of an
Institute of Criminology (Butler, 1975), and in 1961-2 began discussions on establishing a Human (Social) Sciences Research Council.
It again stressed the importance of experiment, description and
measurement in its evidence to the Royal Commission on the Penal
System (1967).
    There can be many criticisms of all these innovations from to-
day's vantage point, but in their time they were significant improvements. If reformers are to be criticized for their work in
the 1950s and 1960s it should rather be for falling into the trap
of concentrating too much on institutional practice, without enough
questioning scrutiny of the underlying principles which should
always be in the forefront of reformers' considerations. In tracing
the evolution of reform methods, the trouble was that the more specialist the League became, the lower it pitched its voice. It continued to submit a steady flow of evidence to official committees
and Advisory Councils; but most of them were buried between the
staid covers of its annual reports - sometimes only in summary, with
the invitation to dedicated seekers after knowledge to apply to the
League's office for the full text.
    Hugh Klare also followed the policy, hitherto moderately success-
ful, of privately corresponding with, and talking to, those with the
power to effect changes (notably Lionel Fox). This proved, however,
to have drawbacks. First, changes that could be brought about by
these methods were limited in the main to those which did not require legislation but depended on administrative action, which in
turn was circumscribed by buildings, money, and staff attitudes.
(But it should not be forgotten that much legislation is drafted by

civil servants.) Second, the public and even the League's own members were scarcely involved. Third, administrative changes at the Home Office had undermined the effectiveness of this form of persuasion. In 1963 the Prison Commissioners, who had enjoyed a considerable amount of autonomy, were absorbed into the Home Office, ostensibly in the name of closer liaison with other departments, and became the Prison Department. Klare foresaw the damper that this would apply on reforming initiative and, with many others, campaigned strenuously against the take-over. When it proved impossible to prevent, he recommended that at least the new Department should have a clearly defined top job (Howard League, 1967). This was done, but the advantage was soon undermined by the civil service practice of ensuring versatility in its senior staff by frequent transfers, thus reinforcing their tendency to concentrate on immediate problems such as security and staff shortages, rather than on the development and implementation of a coherent penal policy; inevitably, some of the career civil servants have not had the long-term commitment to penal ideals which distinguished several of their forerunners at the Prison Commission. It is striking that while there were only six chairmen of the Commission between 1921 and 1963, there were five chairmen of the Prisons Board between 1964 and 1973 (not counting Sir Arthur Peterson, who had held the Commission chairmanship). It is difficult, as Alice in Wonderland might have said, to hold a conversation with a person who keeps changing into someone else.

In all consideration of what reformers achieved, or failed to achieve, it should be remembered that three further main strands ran continuously through their work. One was the abolition of the death penalty, to which many members of the Howard League and the National Campaign for the Abolition of the Death Penalty devoted considerable time and effort right up to the final abolition in 1969, and even afterwards, for example to counter attempts in 1974-5 to bring back the death penalty for acts of terrorism. This was a concerted campaign involving the whole gamut of reform techniques: lobbying of members of both Houses of Parliament, original research (notably by Terence Morris and Louis Blom-Cooper (1964)), the collection of a large number of influential signatures, besides pamphlets, articles, letters to the press, briefing of radio and television producers, and other means of persuasion. It was a long-drawn-out process, but had the merit of being so thorough as to make the restorationists' case difficult to sustain. First, although Cicely Craven's attempt to include abolition in the 1948 Criminal Justice Act was deflected for tactical reasons into the appointment of a Royal Commission, the latter's Report (1953) when it appeared was exhaustive and convincing. Then the compromise Homicide Act 1957 proved the unworkability of partial abolition. And Parliament showed by supporting abolition on a free vote in 1965 and, finally, in 1969, that a majority of informed opinion was now firmly opposed to capital punishment.

The second strand has been the Howard League's international work. In 1928 it had presented a request for an International Convention for the Treatment of Prisoners, and Margery Fry afterwards presented proposals which were eventually adopted as the United Nations Standard Minimum Rules in 1955. Hugh Klare continued the international tradition. In 1956-7 he helped to persuade the Social

Defence section of the UN to maintain its programme of quinquennial congresses, and in 1959-61 he was seconded to the Council of Europe's Department of Criminology.

Third, there has been the continuing effort to 'educate the public'. Speakers were provided for schools and other organizations, and the Howard League runs its own series of meetings and summer schools. It gave, and continues to give, background information to journalists ('A leading article in "The Times" accurately reflects your Executive Committee's misgivings about the working of the Court of Criminal Appeal', as one Annual Report (1956-7) discreetly put it) and to students and schoolchildren requesting help with the 'projects' which are increasingly fashionable in educational circles. It also publishes its annual 'Howard Journal', which tries to provide an international perspective in non-specialist language.

But during the debate in the late 1960s on such topics as conditions in maximum security prisons, allegations of brutality in detention centres, the abolition of dietary punishment, and the increased use of non-custodial measures - all subjects of great importance - the prison population was steadily climbing. It was left to RAP to ask the brash question 'Is it right to incarcerate people at all?'

Radical Alternatives to Prison was formed on 8 October 1970, to carry on from a moribund body started in the 1960s, the Prison Reform Council. It is different from the Howard League in its whole approach and style. In place of formal council and working parties, it has informal groups. Howard League pronouncements tended to be addressed to informed opinion and specifically the Home Office, and were phrased accordingly: it suggested, for example, that borstal trainees 'might possibly' have choice in their clothing (which, incidentally, they now have). But RAP speaks directly to its public ('All offenders must remain within the community'; 'RAP demands...'). While the Howard League conscientiously considered that 'nothing is easier than merely to denounce prison conditions' (Howard League, 1958) but a responsible reforming body must propose directions for improvement, RAP went ahead and denounced them. Hugh Klare had probably been right in thinking that the general public did not care how prisoners were treated, but RAP showed that a section of the public cared very much when made aware of the facts.

To demand abolition without proposing alternatives, as advocated by Mathiesen (1974), may well be the best method in some cases; but the tactics he advocates, using the example of abolishing imprisonment for vagrants, would not necessarily apply to offenders who are perceived as presenting a greater risk to the public. Even Mathiesen acknowledges the ambiguity which obliges an abolitionist organization like KROM to work for some reforms of a non-abolishing kind, such as raising prisoners' wages, partly to make things better for prisoners and partly to demonstrate to them its concern for their needs.

RAP may be criticized for oversimplification, for the impracticability of some of its schemes, and for its refusal to attempt to improve prisoners' conditions, on the ground that that would, so to speak, be giving diplomatic recognition to an unfriendly regime. (Some members felt that reform was laudable, but best left to other

organizations (RAP, 1973b); but this point of view does not often
emerge in RAP pronouncements.) But at that time, when the prison
population and the length of sentences were both rising, this extreme position was effective in bringing reformers back to first
principles, and making them reflect on the implications of the fact
that the treadwheel, and corporal and capital punishment, were all
once considered as justifiable as prison is to-day (Wright, 1973).

RAP may also in some of its pronouncements have reinforced the
prejudices of those who accuse reformers of mollycoddling criminals
and ignoring their victims. The danger of stating uncompromising
ideals is incomprehension or rejection by the traditionally minded;
the danger of trying to keep on their wave-length is that the mes-
sage may get watered down.

Organization in RAP has been based on what Donald Schon (1971)
calls the 'Johnny Appleseed' movement: travelling round the country, telling of the new ideas, and encouraging groups to form. To
that extent it has been quite successful. But some of the groups
lacked the bourgeois apparatus of chairman, secretary and agenda, a
lack which in extreme cases could have stultifying results:

> The group has been going for two years. The first year it was a
> 'talk shop'. Good attendance, but not stable, so they were con-
> stantly reiterating RAP's aims and having the same arguments with
> different people....Eventually it split into three groups:
> 1. 'Radical' radical group held a one-day talk in and set a date
> for abolition of all prisons. Then the group disintegrated...
> (RAP, 1973b).

The other groups, however, started potentially constructive projects, and showed that the loosely-knit, informal approach can
successfully involve a large number of people actively in the work
of the movement, and inspire a wide variety of initiatives. Activities include street theatre, compilation of a book, and handing out
of leaflets at Labour party conferences.

Some of the strengths and weaknesses of RAP's methods are frankly
assessed in Richard Hartnoll's account of the Holloway campaign (RAP
1973b). The issue of imprisoning women had been chosen as a telling
example by which to explain to the public the damage inseparable
from imprisonment, and a pamphlet (RAP, 1972) presented the case
against the rebuilding of Holloway prison, then in its early stages
(Faulkner, 1971). Groups of volunteers helped with research for the
report, which was widely publicized and well received. There was a
not-so-successful meeting in Central Hall, Westminster; and 'things
then ground to a halt'. Hartnoll comments that the campaign group
had seen the publication of the report as an end in itself rather
than as the beginning of a campaign, and was not sure whether to aim
at stopping the rebuilding altogether (the alternative would presumably be to propose that it should be built but made over to male
prisoners or to mental patients, either of which RAP would be reluctant to advocate).

Meanwhile RAP is experimenting with the demonstration-project
approach; it has recently begun a project in North London to
'divert' people from the criminal justice system (RAP, 1973a, 1975).
(It is an interesting sidelight on the effects of dividing responsibility within the Home Office for the treatment of offenders that
RAP should obtain support from the Probation and After-Care Depart-

ment while its relations with the Prison Department are still very sensitive.)

In 1972 the public heard a new set of initials, PROP, which stands for Preservation of the Rights of Prisoners. It had been planned by two prisoners while in Dartmoor, Douglas Curtis and Dick Pooley, who aimed to persuade inmates to use their tactical advantage that prisons cannot function without their compliance. After a number of passive sit-down demonstrations in prison yards and on roofs, they called a national one-day prison strike on 4 August. Thousands of prisoners joined in. A few mainly young and radical academics gave active moral support, but neither they nor the ex-prisoner spokesmen succeeded in deflecting the attention of the mass media from the disturbances· to the substance of the prisoners' demands which were, in the main, for moderate and overdue reforms (Taylor, 1972). They included the right to trade union membership; to institute legal proceedings without Home Office consent; to legal representation in internal disciplinary proceedings, and press access to these; to parole if certain criteria are met; to communicate freely to press and public; and to adequate preparation for discharge ('Howard Journal', 1973).

Prison staff, however, felt strongly threatened by the demands and by the militant tactics, especially when there was talk of a three-day stoppage and a mass walk-out from open prisons; they threatened to strike themselves unless tough action was taken. The Prison Department responded by disciplining prisoners, and by giving currency to allegations that some prisoners participated only under duress. The charge against the Department is not fabrication - no doubt some such incidents did take place - but one-sidedness. Certainly the staff attitude is important, but prisoners, too, may legitimately have a point of view; but the Department never showed, in public at any rate, that it appreciated this, nor did it insist that the staff should do so.

At this point it seemed to moderates that the leadership of the prisoners was playing into the hands of hard-liners. They had reservations about the desirability of a prisoners' union unless all attempts at creating a collaborative model failed, on the ground that a union/management system involves built-in confrontation ('Howard Journal', 1974). They therefore urged PROP to stop issuing strike threats, and the Prison Department to introduce some of the improvements asked for, and take this last chance to set up its own effective machinery by which prisoners and staff could participate in mutual discussion of problems before they reached crisis proportions (Wright and Gordon, 1972). PROP did stop threatening, but the Prison Department, while introducing a few material improvements, took up an embattled position. In its vocabulary the word 'management' was almost drowned by 'control', 'subversives', 'punishment' and, it is fair to add, 'rewards' - but the latter are apparently being thought of more as incentives to institutional good behaviour than as a preparation for release. Prison officers generally took up a tough stance, partly because of traditional attitudes, but also because they resented being told not to use forcible methods of dispersing demonstrations, when they had received no adequate training in more modern methods of man-management. They justifiably felt that they were placed in a physically exposed position by this half-

policy; they were already thin on the ground, as a result of inten-
sified security arrangements and of the increasing number of penal
establishments, and this was aggravated by a drastic fall in recruitment. There was much hostility to PROP, and to some extent
RAP, and the Prison Department acquiesced in blacklisting both
groups. This went to absurd lengths: in November 1972 Prison Department personnel received a high-level prohibition from attending
a conference on prisoners' rights sponsored by two law lords, a
privy councillor and members of parliament, on the grounds that PROP
and RAP would be represented, and in 1973 Douglas Curtis, then employed by the Home-Office-financed organization NACRO, was refused
admission to Norwich prison by the Prison Officers' Association,
despite Home Office attempts at intervention.

PROP is at present fragmented, but an active group in London is
seeking the sympathy of trades unions, especially on the grounds
that prisoners, as prisons are increasingly industrialized, should
be paid an industrial wage ('Guardian', 1974). It has not been
using prison demonstrations as a tactic, but is trying to apply
pressure from the outside, in particular by publishing detailed allegations of bad conditions and malpractices in prisons (e.g.
Stratton, 1973), in the hope of stirring the authorities to take
action either against the abuses or against PROP. The Home Office,
however, has not openly taken notice of the more extreme allegations, probably because even if they were partly or wholly disproved,
the publicity would be very damaging to prison service morale.
Meanwhile inmate consultative committees have been set up in a few
more prisons; some improvements have been made in such matters as
visiting, permitting personal radios, and the abolition of dietary
punishment, but much bitterness and many petty restrictions remain.

A comparison with events in Sweden is interesting. There, prisoners used the more drastic weapon of the mass hunger strike. Ex-
prisoners worked closely with liberal-minded academics and others,
in the pressure group KRUM, and seem to have secured more public
discussion than in this country of the underlying issues. After
hard negotiations the prisoners secured important concessions including the right to collective bargaining. Not the least of the differences between the two countries is that a senior Swedish prison
administrator felt able to publish a blow-by-blow account of the
negotiations (Marnell, 1974).

Thus in Sweden authority made concessions to democracy; but as
A. Morris (1972) has commented, while reformers may want prisons to
be more effective, prisoners want them to be more humane. If the
authorities intend to run what they consider to be a constructive
regime, they should retain the initiative by introducing it before
prisoners realize the power they have to demand what they, themselves, want.

One practical method of bringing reforms about is a partnership
between a government department and a voluntary organization. NACRO
(National Association for the Care and Resettlement of Offenders) is
largely funded by the Home Office. Originally an 'umbrella' organization servicing other voluntary bodies working mainly with ex-
offenders, it is now engaged in setting up a range of projects such
as LANCE, providing help for single homeless people in the Manches-
ter area, and the New Careers scheme in Bristol, by which young men

who would otherwise have been sent to borstal are trained for jobs
in the social services. These enterprises are specifically designed
not, like the old after-care hostels, to mitigate the effects of the
penal system, but to change it, by showing that for many people
prison can and should be avoided altogether. The projects are to be
evaluated and, if they are successful, used as a lever to press the
authorities to establish more of a similar kind. Hence they must be
included in the category of penal reform. NACRO also undertakes
some traditional reformist activities, such as sponsoring working
parties and organizing conferences.

The question is inevitably asked whether some or all of these
organizations ought to combine; but at least some of the arguments
for separation seem to have merit. There is a case for having (a) a
voluntary organization undertaking demonstration projects, with more
freedom for 'way-out' experiments than is feasible for a government
department, but receiving substantial government grants to relieve
it of precarious and time-consuming dependence on fund-raising;
(b) a think-tank, independent not only of the government but of the
exigencies of day-to-day management of projects, but including prac-
titioners among its members and maintaining informal links with
ministers and civil servants to ensure that its proposals and criticisms are reasonably well informed; (c) a radical group concerned
more with ideals than with 'the art of the possible', and under no
obligation to use 'respectable' methods if it feels that civility to
civil servants and politicians does not produce results; and (d) a
group run by and for ex-offenders, especially ex-prisoners. That is
approximately what we have in NACRO, the Howard League, RAP and
PROP; there are also a few others. Reform is more likely to result
if their activities are co-ordinated; just as in the early nineteenth century there was a need both for total opponents of capital
punishment and for those who secured its progressive elimination,
so now with imprisonment. In this respect the recent record is not
so encouraging. In the autumn of 1974 the Home Office disclosed the
opening of a control unit, a new regime for prisoners described as
persistently disruptive. A relative of one of the first men to be
sent there visited the Howard League, and subsequently the 'Sunday
Times' newspaper; when the details were published all four organizations, together with the National Council for Civil Liberties and
some small groups of ex-prisoners and prisoners' families, formed an
action group. This achieved some publicity and lobbying and, partly
perhaps as a result, control units were all but abandoned; but just
as it was being proposed that the group should continue to work together for other objects, some of the members took exception to published statements by another member, and this led to the group's
disbandment. Part of the underlying reason may have been a difference in attitudes and styles of operation; part may also have been
simply that the individuals concerned did not personally know each
other well enough.

The picture represented by the penal system on the eve of the last
quarter of the twentieth century is a very mixed one. Custodial
establishments are in a demoralized state, partly, it must be said,
because of the activities of their critics. Many of the criticisms
are recognized as valid, but those within the system are obliged to

soldier on, with no tenable official or judicial philosophy to
guide them. Nor have the reformers, enthusiastically proposing ways
of getting people out of prison, taken time to suggest in any detail
what they think should be done with, or to, or for those who remain
inside; perhaps for fear of seeming to acquiesce in the existence
of those unpopular institutions, although even RAP has conceded that
'some must be confined as long as they are likely to harm human
beings' (RAP, 1971, p.27), and other reformers recognise that there
must be a transition period before the hoped-for time when the
prison population reaches its irreducible minimum. In young offenders' establishments, however, there has been somewhat greater official readiness to experiment, even in advance of the long-awaited
report of the Advisory Council on the Penal System (1974); and in
the non-custodial sector new ideas are gradually beginning to sprout.
What should reformers be doing at a time like this?

Their first task is a conceptual one: to get away from using the
old yardsticks of prison, punishment and deterrence, and look at the
basic problem of deciding what behaviour society should forbid, or
discourage, and what methods are effective, permissible, and practi-
cable. This puts them in a position of perpetual compromise. The
social injustices and personal shortcomings (of the transgressor
himself and those directly or indirectly responsible for his environment) which often underlie deviant behaviour cannot be eradicated
over-night; methods of controlling behaviour are not (and let us
hope never will be) totally effective. But living together in a
complex society is possible only if certain standards of conduct are
maintained. The need is to explore ways of doing so: for example,
by recognizing that punishment is only one possible way of discouraging actions which are not tolerated, and not necessarily an effective one; by making sure that everyone is capable of conforming to
the required code; and by giving everyone the opportunity to contribute, according to his talents, to the well-being of himself, his
family and the community. Traditional methods must be measured
against these standards; improvements proposed; and where the new
methods depend on public attitudes, these must be changed. But at
the same time, while old methods persist, they must be constantly
reviewed and pressure applied for the removal of their worst features.

They ought also to face up to the problem of those who, rightly
or wrongly, will continue to be detained: the dilemma between 'containment' and treatment. People should not be sent to prison for
treatment, yet while there is an indeterminate element prisons have
an obligation to enable them to be released as soon as possible.
This could do much to clarify both sentencing aims and prison
staff's conception of their task. Meanwhile, however, the very
principle of indeterminate sentences is being challenged (N. Morris,
1975), and this, too, needs to be resolved.

Second, background work must continue, with emphasis as always on
the collection of facts. This means promoting research that is
oriented towards reform, or more precisely towards the constant
testing of assumptions - both the old and hide-bound and the new and
starry-eyed. The 'poverty lobby' has shown the enormous advantage
in such work of a strong base among academics, and penal reformers
would be well-advised to establish an equally strong base in the

universities. Information also needs to be collected and collated
through official channels and from social workers, ex-offenders, and
others with first-hand experience. Official secrecy should be opposed. Then the reformers can formulate their own policies. Working
parties can still be an effective method: witness the one set up by
Justice, the Howard League and NACRO to consider how to enable people
to 'live down' a criminal conviction incurred many years previously.
Its report was published in 1972, and in 1974 skilful campaigning
overcame opposition and secured the passage of the Rehabilitation of
Offenders Act.

Meanwhile education of the public must continue by all the usual
means: conferences, articles, news items and so on. Supporters of
reform need to persuade more people working in the mass media of the
social importance of social control: if the number of pointless
prison sentences received the same publicity as, say, the number of
battered wives and children, some progress might be made. Reformers
cannot do it all themselves: they need the help of writers and producers.

There should be continuing informed public debate, such as that
initiated by Dr Roger Hood and Lord Justice Scarman in 1974. It
should not consist entirely of fault-finding, but should draw attention to promising new methods; especially in prisons, where staff
may be demoralized (to the detriment of prisoners) by constant criticism, and measures in the community, which are apt to be misunder-
stood by the public. In addition, as Klare (1974) has commented, it
is time to form local groups and involve the grass roots. The treatment of offenders is a more complex subject than some others, because the object of concern is considered by most people as 'unde-
serving' while some see him, in part, as a 'victim' of the social
system; moreover there is much debate over the processes by which
he is defined, let alone what should be done with (or for) him when
he has been identified. Despite all this, reformers should not
baulk at the attempt to show the public the fundamental importance
of the methods society uses to try to prevent people from harming
each other, or the community, or (in some cases) themselves, and the
pitfalls involved. Campaigning of this kind may even help with the
chronic problem of fund-raising. Reformers must maintain the integ-
rity of their principles, but if they go too far ahead of public
opinion the public will not merely disagree but will fail even to
understand their arguments. Morris (1972, pp.5-6) has pointed out
that many ordinary people hold to a simple belief in retribution,
and its rationalization deterrence, as the right basis for a penal
system; and Field (1974) stresses yet again that this attitude
needs to be combated by facts. He also comments that the popular
press preserves a stereotype of reformers as 'lenient', 'on the side
of the offender but forgetting the victim' (though the quality
papers and radio and television programmes are more balanced), and
spokesmen of reform organizations will have to develop techniques of
living down this reputation. They should also use discrimination in
public attacks on each other: it is hard enough to draft a statement intended to impinge on moderate to hard-liners, without having
to look over one's shoulder at ultra-radicals ready to score debating points.

An information centre on crime and the treatment of offenders is

urgently needed, as the Howard League has already informally proposed to the Home Office. It could provide an interdisciplinary
forum for the exchange of views among social workers, probation
officers, prison staff, residential child care workers, police, magistrates, academics, judges and administrators; it could offer
training, perhaps also on an interdisciplinary basis, to supplement
what is officially provided; and it could serve as a resource to
Citizens' Advice Bureaux, law centres, and others who offer legal
advice to offenders, including prisoners, and their families. In
this connection it is perhaps time for a restructuring of the work
of the Institute for the Study and Treatment of Delinquency and the
Howard Centre (a small offshoot of the Howard League which for several years ran courses in group dynamics). All these activities
would have the useful by-product of adding to the sum of available
information, which, it is worth remembering, is not merely a stick
to beat the authorities with, but a (partial) safeguard against ill-
informed criticism and reforms that are inadequately conceived or
executed.

The next, and crucial, task is to secure changes. The value of
demonstration projects has already been stressed. They should help
to promote a healthy climate of opinion because the results of new
projects, where both staff and participants are on their mettle, are
usually good - perhaps the most effective system would be one con-
sisting entirely of a succession of innovations.

It will then be up to the reformers to see that this atmosphere
spreads to the courts, for example by persuading them to extend the
scope of their sentencing conferences to include more consideration
of the effects of their sentences. Should this approach fail, le-
gislators will have to be persuaded to take action to restrict
courts' powers, as they have in the past.

Those changes which do not require legislation may be introduced
by administrators, if they are confident of public support; fail-
ing that, they need to be able to count on political backing, or to
be pressed to take action by ministers who are willing to accept
responsibility. Here again, the implications for reformers are
clear.

The importance of structure should not be overlooked. The Webbs
were aware of it (1922, pp.243 ff) when they pointed out that 'Local
inspection of central government administration will always be less
effective than a centrally organized inspection of local government
administration.' Klare, following his earlier opposition to the
winding up of the Prison Commission, has now suggested (1973, ch.16)
that apart from broad policy and legislation the administration of
the penal system as a whole should be integrated and removed from
ministerial responsibility and from the Home Office. Similarly, Mr
Leo Abse has recently proposed that there should be a Youth Authority for all aspects of the treatment of young offenders (Advisory
Council on the Penal System, 1974). The Prison Department itself
is aware of it, in its insistence on creating the right management
structure and giving prison officers experience of participation
before expecting them to operate a system in which participation is
extended to inmates. It does not, however, seem to have overcome
the problems of an over-centralized structure. Another pattern
which the Howard League has suggested for the Prison Department, and

which could be productive in probation and non-custodial treatment
also, is what Schon (1971, p.147) calls the 'propose-dispose'
arrangement, which uses the incentive of allocations of money not to
individuals but to agencies. The central office formulates broad
specifications, solicits proposals from local agents, allocates
funds and withholds funds from those who fall short. There are pitfalls, as Schon points out, but the Probation Subsidy scheme in
California (Smith, 1972) and other states shows that it can stimu-
late ideas and, incidentally, save money. The nearest approximation
in this country is probably the Urban Aid scheme; the Probation and
After-Care Department of the Home Office have a small fund of the
same kind, but it is unpublicized and hence loses half its point,
which is the stimulation of ideas. The Department also missed
chances to introduce this principle in 1973 and 1974, when it increased the central grant for general and training purposes respectively, without first inviting local Probation and After-Care Committees to suggest what innovations they would introduce with the
money. This idea has been proposed again by the Howard League
(1975) as a means of funding the resources needed to keep more young
adult offenders in the community and out of institutions. Alterations to the structure may produce results where exhortation and
confrontation fail. To a limited extent a system can build in its
own reforming element, for example by ensuring that the official
channels of communication really work (preferably with alternative
parallel routes), and by setting up a body like the Advisory Council
on the Penal System which has sufficient independence to present an
alternative to the official view. To concentrate on structure is a
safeguard against reformers' too-specific solutions which sometimes
prove to be misguided.

In choosing its methods, a campaigning body has to choose care-
fully between various tactics. One of these is whether to try to
remain on friendly terms with civil servants, at the risk of having
its moral indignation blunted by too great an awareness of the practical obstacles which always loom much larger to those who have to
contend with them every day, and the vigour of its public statements
sapped by personal acquaintanceship with those responsible for the
policies under attack. Should they accept confidential information
'off the record', which they may then not be able to use openly?
About 1957, Mrs Huws Jones says, 'According to some angry young men,
the League was in the pocket of the Home Office. (But) Margery Fry
was unshaken. She had known over years the quality of her friends
in the Prison Commission: Maurice Waller, Alexander Paterson, Lionel Fox. Though when she looked around everything remained to do,
when she looked back the changes were enormous' (1966, p.236). The
Howard League's Annual Report for 1958-9 takes up the theme, stres-
sing the importance of

> the informal exchange of information and views with officials of
> all kinds, from those in the Home Office and in the Prison Com-
> mission to probation officers, approved school personnel and
> prison officers. These informal contacts have increased con-
> siderably in recent years and have proved of the greatest poss-
> ible value, both in getting to know the detailed problems and
> difficulties which are met, and in making known and discussing
> the League's own suggestions and views, themselves shaped by the
> knowledge and understanding gained in these discussions.

(The Report goes on to refer to the value of contacts with the offenders themselves.) Liaison with officialdom can be taken too far, but on balance it is probably best that at least one of the reforming organizations should maintain open lines of communication, because information is the most valuable commodity in the reform business, and there are generally ways of using it 'without attribution' or eliciting it through overt channels, for example by prompting a parliamentary question. A relationship which allows a reform group entry to prisons and receipt of unpublished documents is of great value; and the tradition of public debate in this country allows views to be expressed forcibly but without rancour.

Another dilemma is the recurring problem of closed institutions: allegations of malpractice, including cruelty. The person or organization hearing these is in a quandary. For one thing, to take up a case on the full scale can be very time-consuming. To secure corroboration is difficult. If the recipient of the complaint is convinced that there are at least serious grounds for disquiet, he must choose between various alternatives. He can publish all he knows, like PROP, but this may generate more resentment than reform. He can demand an official (if possible public) inquiry. It is, however, very difficult to secure enough evidence even to make the case for holding one; perhaps this is as well, because if the inquiry ended inconclusively with inmates telling one story and staff another, more harm than good might be done. In other types of institution, such as mental subnormality hospitals, the conclusive information has generally come from young or probationary staff not too tied by group loyalty or career prospects (and, when one can interest individual journalists in the subject, they can also often be a valuable source of information). It is extremely unfortunate for the health of penal institutions that those who might have the courage to speak out are subject to the additional threat of prosecution under the Official Secrets Act; even chaplains (Wright, 1974). Probably the best course, in the absence of strong evidence, is to approach the authorities, without making more allegations than the evidence bears out, and ask for their version of the story. This seldom results in an admission of error, but lets the authorities know that the veil of secrecy has been penetrated; the hope is that they will quietly issue new instructions or move offending personnel. When staff were in fact not at fault, or do not recognize that they were, a discreet approach can avoid reinforcing their conviction that reformers are ill-informed and over-critical, and adding to their feelings of insecurity which can be vented on inmates. It can also happen (Howard League, 1973, pp.2-3) that the authorities tacitly concede that some 'excessive force' was used, but in the prevailing tension (which by implication is blamed on the prisoners) are unwilling to undermine staff morale by reproving them, still less by inflicting the trauma of a full inquiry.

Again, the ultimate solution might well lie in an improved structure with a self-correcting system, where problems were dealt with as part of a regular routine in which everyone participated, without waiting till they reached crisis proportions and required emergency measures. Similarly, there should be pressure towards professional status for staff, so that they themselves would take part in management and be concerned to maintain standards, rather

than be tempted on occasion to band together against the management
to protect sub-standard colleagues.

It may be possible to devise completely new techniques for reform.
For example Grant (CIBA, 1973, pp.184ff) describes how the problem
of citizen-police conflicts was tackled, not by pressing for an
independent complaints tribunal but through research. He selected a
group of police officers with a record of 'incidents', encouraged
them to discuss the problem among themselves and, with a minimum of
guidance from him, to work out their own new methods of handling
various types of situation. In Britain, the Department of Health
and Social Security runs seminars on violence for mixed groups of
residential and non-residential social workers, together with administrators. The Information Centre (see above, pp.99-100) could be
developed in a similar direction.

Other decisions await the reformers. Should they take an active
part in negotiations, for example by announcing that unless a satisfactory official alternative arrangement is introduced, they will
support prisoners' demands for collective negotiation? Is there any
future in legal action on the American model, in discovering ways in
which the system contravenes the law and securing court orders to
comply? The Legal Advice and Assistance Act may enable prisoners,
and for that matter people subject to non-custodial measures, to
obtain lawyers' support in challenging arbitrary administrative decisions. They will be encouraged by the case of Golder, a prisoner
who successfully applied to the European Court of Human Rights. The
Court held, in 1975, that the European Convention had been breached
when he was refused permission to contact a lawyer and his letters,
in which he attempted to do so, were stopped. The British Government has changed some of its practices accordingly. It can also be
argued that some administrative decisions, in which the offender is
not allowed satisfactory representation, deprive him of human rights
(Borrie, 1974); this too could be tested in the courts. In deciding which of these methods to use, the reform organizations are subject to various constraints, especially financial ones. One is that
under present law a body which engaged in too overt activity of a
kind that can be described as 'political' could be deprived of its
charitable status and the concomitant tax concessions.

Another is that voluntary organizations are particularly vulnerable to inflation; since there are limits to the amount by which
they can increase their membership subscriptions, they must devote a
considerable amount of effort to attracting new members. This means
that they must be seen to be active, and that they are placed under
a strong temptation to concentrate on those activities which bring
publicity, whether or not they are the most likely to bring about
reforms: for example, in choosing between the press statement and
the meeting behind closed doors. Similarly with the other large
source of revenue, the grant-giving trusts. Many (but fortunately
not all - the Howard League has recently obtained two grants for
limited periods, and RAP has had considerable support from Christian
Action) trustees like to give to specific projects rather than to
general expenses, and they are reluctant to undertake commitments of
indeterminate length. If, to take an extreme example, the Howard
League felt that its best contribution would be to concentrate every
resource into a major blueprint for the maintenance of pro-social

behaviour, it would probably lose members through not being seen to be active, and the project might be impossible unless a trust could be persuaded to underwrite the whole cost. The pressures are not irresistible, but they exist. Another solution is NACRO's: to accept official help in promoting reform. But while this method has obvious potential in getting things done, there is still a need for an on-going independent appraisal of principles, free from the day-to-day pressures of managing projects; and it would be wrong for the voice of reformers to be heard only through an organization that is mainly dependent on government finance, unless a system is devised which can be seen to be entirely free from 'strings': the grants given by the government's Voluntary Services Unit appear to meet this criterion.

The ultimate test of the reformers is their basic humane philosophy. They need not only to be devising a new system, but should remember those who are still caught up in the old. Nor should they discuss the structure of the penal system without considering also the structure of society (Jefferson and Clarke, 1974). Administrators and politicians, quite apart from political and organizational pressures, are often too busy dealing with everyday crises to be able to formulate underlying principles and relate them to long-term social aims (though the Home Office's new Crime Policy Planning Unit is potentially a valuable step in that direction). It is vital that the reform societies are not forced to become equally preoccupied with the problem of staying in existence. A membership subscription to any one of them costs a few pence a week. The rest is in the hands of the public.

REFERENCES

ADVISORY COUNCIL ON THE PENAL SYSTEM (1974), 'Young Adult Offenders' (Chairman: Sir Kenneth Younger), HMSO, London.
BARRY, JOHN VINCENT (1958), 'Alexander Maconochie of Norfolk Island' Oxford University Press, Melbourne and New York.
BENNEY, MARK (1948), 'Gaol Delivery', Longmans, London.
BORRIE, GORDON (1974), The Prisoner's status in parole decision making, in D.A. Thomas, ed., 'Parole', Institute of Criminology, Cambridge.
BUTLER, LORD (1974), The foundation of the Institute of Criminology in Cambridge, in Roger Hood, ed., 'Crime, Criminology and Public Policy', Heinemann, London.
CIBA (1973), 'Medical Care of Prisoners and Detainees', Elsevier-Excempta Medica - North Holland, Amsterdam.
FAULKNER, D.E.R. (1971), The redevelopment of Holloway prison, 'Howard Journal', 13(2).
FIELD, FRANK (1974), The politics of penal reform, 'Christian Action Journal', Winter 1973-4.
FOX, SIR LIONEL W. (1952), 'The English Prison and Borstal Systems', Routledge & Kegan Paul, London.
'Guardian' (1974), 29 January, p.5.
HOBHOUSE, STEPHEN and BROCKWAY, FENNER (1922), 'English Prisons Today', Longmans, London.
HOOD, ROGER (1974), 'Toleránce and the tariff', NACRO, London.

'Howard Journal' (1973), Editorial, 13(4), pp.264-6.
'Howard Journal' (1974), Editorial, 14(1), p.3.
HOWARD LEAGUE FOR PENAL REFORM (1948), 'Annual Report', 1947-8.
HOWARD LEAGUE FOR PENAL REFORM (1958), Executive committee minutes (unpublished).
HOWARD LEAGUE FOR PENAL REFORM (1967), 'Annual Report', 1966-7.
HOWARD LEAGUE FOR PENAL REFORM (1972), 'Granting bail in Magistrates' Courts'.
HOWARD LEAGUE FOR PENAL REFORM (1973), 'Annual Report', 1972-3.
HOWARD LEAGUE FOR PENAL REFORM (1974), 'Ill-founded Premisses: The Logic of Penal Policy and the Prison Building Programme'.
HOWARD LEAGUE FOR PENAL REFORM (1975), 'Between Probation and Custody: Young Adult Offenders'.
JEFFERSON, TONY and CLARKE, J. (1974), Down these mean streets: the meaning of mugging, 'Howard Journal',14(1), pp.37-53.
JENKINS, ROY (1974), at AGM of the Central Council of Probation and After-Care Committees, 21 May.
JONES, E. HUWS (1966), 'Margery Fry: The Essential Amateur', Oxford University Press, London.
JUSTICE, HOWARD LEAGUE and NACRO (1972), 'Living it Down: The Problem of Old Convictions', Stevens, London.
JUSTICE, HOWARD LEAGUE and NACRO (1975), 'Boards of Visitors in Penal Institutions' (Chairman: Lord Jellicoe), Barry Rose, Chichester.
KLARE, HUGH (1973), 'People in Prison', Pitman, London.
KLARE, HUGH (1974), Private communication.
MACKENNA, SIR BRIAN (1973), 'Sentencing and Penal Polidy', Paper to Howard League Summer School, 11 September: reported in 'The Times', 12 September: published in Louis Blom-Cooper, ed., 'The Future of the Penal System', Oxford University Press.
MARNELL, GUNNAR (1974), Penal reform: a Swedish viewpoint, 'Howard Journal', 14(1), pp.8-21.
MATHIESEN, T. (1974), The Politics of Abolition, 'Scandinavian Studies in Criminology' (4), Martin Robertson, London.
MORRIS, A. (1972), Correctional reform: illusion and reality, 'Correctional research', (22).
MORRIS, NORVAL (1975), 'The Future of Imprisonment', Chicago University Press, Chicago and London.
MORRIS, TERENCE and BLOM-COOPER, LOUIS (1964), 'A Calendar of Murder', Michael Joseph, London.
PLAYFAIR, GILES (1971), 'The Punitive Obsession', Gollancz, London.
RAP (Radical Alternatives to Prison) (1971), 'The Case for Radical Alternatives to Prison'.
RAP (1972), 'Alternatives to Holloway'.
RAP (1973a), 'Project Outline for a North London Alternatives Project based on One London Court'.
RAP (1973b), Report of a RAP national meeting held at Bristol.
RAP (1975), 'Newham Alternatives Project'.
REPORT OF HOME OFFICE COMMITTEE ON PRISONS (1895), (Chairman: Herbert Gladstone), C.7702.
REPORT OF THE ROYAL COMMISSION ON CAPITAL PUNISHMENT (1949-53), (Chairman: Sir Ernest Gowers), Cmd 8932.
ROSE, GORDON (1961), 'The Struggle for Penal Reform', Stevens, London.

ROYAL COMMISSION ON THE PENAL SYSTEM IN ENGLAND AND WALES (1967), Minutes of evidence taken before the Royal Commission, HMSO, London.
SCARMAN, SIR LESLIE (1974), 'Control of Sentencing: The Balance between the Judge and the Executive', Howard League, London.
SCHON, DONALD A. (1971), 'Beyond the Stable State', Temple Smith, London.
SMITH, ROBERT L. (1972), 'A Quiet Revolution' (US Department of Health, Education and Welfare), US GPO, Washington.
STRATTON, BRIAN (1973), 'Who guards the Guards?' PROP, London.
TAYLOR, LAURIE (1972), Prison splash, 'New Society', 28 September, pp.618-20.
WEBB, BEATRICE (1926), 'My Apprenticeship', Longmans, London.
WEBB, BEATRICE and WEBB, SIDNEY (1922), 'English Prisons under Local Government', Longmans, London.
WRIGHT, MARTIN (1973), To keep people in prison or to keep them out? 'The Times', 8 February.
WRIGHT, MARTIN (1974), The church and the offender, 'St Margaret the Queen, Streatham, Parish Magazine', February.
WRIGHT, MARTIN and GORDON, J. (1972), Prison life: confrontation or co-operation? 'The Times', 31 August.
YOUNGER, SIR KENNETH (1973), 'On the Judiciary' (Chairman's address to Howard League AGM).

Chapter 8

FUTURE PROSPECTS OF IMPRISONMENT IN BRITAIN

Seán McConville

Continuously from the late eighteenth century there have been attempts to use prisons as places of penal treatment. Indeed, the treatment goal is definitive of modern imprisonment. Since the Gladstone Report of 1895 the pursuit of effective reformatory and rehabilitative methods has been a central endeavour of policy-makers, reformers and administrators. This article will argue that the reformatory use of imprisonment is based on assumptions of doubtful validity; that treatment objectives and their techniques are not open to empirical assessment; and that the time has come for a complete abandonment of these objectives in our prisons. Some possible consequences of such a change in policy will be briefly examined.

Despite the widespread use of the word, definitions of 'treatment' do not abound. Even official publications have been disappointingly reluctant to be explicit in their use of the term. The White Paper 'The Adult Offender' (1965), although addressing itself throughout to the problems of treating adult offenders, nowhere explained its understanding of treatment, a deficiency also marked in a previous important policy statement 'Penal Practice in a Changing Society' (1959). In fact, it was not until the publication of 'People in Prison' (1969) that an official definition was given:

No clear distinction can, or should be drawn between the aspects of treatment that are primarily designed to regulate the daily life of an offender in custody and those that look primarily towards his return to the community....Thus it is wrong to think of treatment as an item, or choice of items, that can be added at will to the daily regime of a prison or borstal to meet the needs of offenders. Neither our capacity for the diagnosis of the needs of offenders nor the ability to effect a cure is at present as great as many advocates of this or that form of treatment have implied. We need a view of treatment that embraces all that is done by or for the offender in custody. But there is also a place in the prison system for the use of the term in the alternative sense in which it relates to a diagnosis and to the possibility of a changed way of life; and there are already in the system a wide variety of forms of treatment that have been evolved in the hope that they may directly affect an offender's

> behaviour both in custody and after release and may affect his
> rehabilitation (p.21).

This statement offers us two clearly different concepts of treatment,
emphasizing that in practice it is extremely difficult to distinguish between them. The first use of the term is general, and has
tautologous implications - all that is done to or for an imprisoned
offender. The routines of feeding, clothing, washing and watching
the health of inmates, for example, and the business of maintaining
buildings and grounds and their necessary services. From the official standpoint this form of treatment is not arbitrary: it is regulated specifically and by general concepts of propriety laid down
in rules and standing orders. Primarily and necessarily associated
with operational processes, such treatment has no necessary relationship, or even intended relationship, to the reformatory goal. Some
incidental reformatory connection may be claimed: the argument, for
instance, that an inmate who keeps himself clean and neat will develop thereby certain habits of self-discipline relevant to his resettlement into the community. Thus, with this milieu view of treatment, health and provisioning requirements are the primary objective, but there may be reformatory effects. Of course it can be
argued that institutional maintenance procedures may operate in
another way, and have a non-reformatory effect. But such assessments on either side are usually post-hoc, and speculative, offering no firm evidence for imputations of secondary benefit or damage.
This form of treatment, for reasons of physical and psychological
health, and to meet the security objective, will overwhelmingly
constitute most of the regime of imprisonment.

The second, more narrowly defined concept of treatment, involving
diagnosis and responsive measures, is the central focus of this
article. Treatment and training in this sense must necessarily be
controlled and purposive. At some level there must be a rational,
demonstrable link between individual components of the regime and
the reformatory goal. Although this form of treatment has strong
implications of positive or constructive influence, this is not essential. Punishment is a form of treatment, and may consist of a
series of actions purposively undertaken to inflict pain, in the
interests of general and specific deterrence. It has become conventional in modern times that punishment is not considered to be
reformatory: in the modern English prison system punitive treatment
is explicitly eschewed - except as a response to prison offences.
Therefore, unless otherwise stated, treatment in this article will
refer to reformatory influence, as distinct from punitive pressure.

What then are the components of diagnostic prison treatment;
what are their specific objectives; and upon what evidence is their
efficacy measured? It must first be said that in some institutions
no distinction is drawn between a general regime and specific components of treatment. Paterson's method of borstal training, which
combined the accomplishment of a sound physique by means of a rigorous time-filling routine with psychological pressures exercised by
delegation of authority and the deliberate cultivation of inmate
leadership and peer-group influences, depended on the social climate
of the institution as a whole. Thus although any one component of
the regime could be linked to a specific goal, both means and end
had meaning only in the general context.

Many of Paterson's followers, such as John Vidler, attempted to apply this type of social milieu treatment to prisons, and to institutional routine to meet what they perceived as individual needs. This treatment could have as many variations as there were governors and inmates - as indeed Paterson's individualistic penology demanded. Partly because of poor borstal success rates, and because of the greater critical and analytical ability of the social sciences, generic forms of institutional treatment are now regarded with some scepticism, despite the continued claims made for therapeutic communities in the field of mental health. In retrospect it can be seen that institutional therapy was always somewhat cult-like, requiring and even emphasizing faith in a manner that could only uneasily be accommodated with the agnostic rationality of modern bureaucracy.

Treatment based on a number of distinct and individually justifiable elements is more desirable and acceptable in modern conditions. This is exemplified in some ways by the employment of prison psychologists, whose ranks have grown in number and whose influence within the prison system has also steadily risen. Initially they were employed to assess for the courts and assist in the allocation of prisoners. As an exercise in diagnostic treatment, however, allocation cannot be claimed ever to have had great success. Given the always stretched capacity of the borstals and prisons, and factors such as security, and the requirement of nearness to families for visiting purposes, it is doubtful if allocation involved the matching of offenders' needs and treating institution in more than a tiny minority of cases. In any event allocation was necessarily to prisons operating general regimes, in which individual treatment components were largely indistinguishable from institutional routine. Although psychologists have more and more been used to investigate the treatment needs of certain types of offender, their results have not so far produced scientifically designed effective training schemes. Even the psychiatrically oriented and intensively staffed Grendon prison seems able to claim no greater success than other institutions.

Recent Prison Department reports indicate other possible elements of treatment: in 1972, for example, the report subsumes education and physical education under this heading. In neither case, it is most noticeable, is there any attempt to relate these provisions to particular reformatory needs, which is the critical treatment relationship, no matter what other laudable ends are served. This very point arises in the 1973 report, where the provision of remedial education is presented in terms of general community need. A newspaper comment is cited with some approbation: 'If you were one of the millions of adult illiterates in England and Wales and you wanted to learn to read, you could try a longish term in one of Her Majesty's prisons or borstals. There would be incidental disadvantages, but at least systematic tuition in reading would be readily available' (HMSO, 1974, p.21). Thus it is quite possible, but rather misleading in a section labelled 'treatment', simply to report on how educational facilities and activities have expanded. Although reformatory results are not claimed, the implication is that such provision serves reformatory objectives. As the discussion does not become explicit, the lack of supporting evidence does not become an embarrassment. Similarly neither physical or

vocational training or even constructive leisure activities can be
related concretely to reformatory goals.

Prison industry provides another example of specific treatment.
Over the last decade successive Prison Department reports have noted
with some satisfaction the introduction of 'life-like' work situations. Industrial workshops and even complete industrial prisons
(such as Coldingley) have attempted to replicate the civilian industrial environment. The reports give examples of the replacement of
'low calibre work' (such as mail-bag sewing and telephone dismant-
ling) by more worthwhile industrial activity. Indeed, it has been
pointed out that on the basis of the claim that the best kind of
training is 'economic labour', 'efficient industry seems to have
taken precedence over the training and other aims of the prison'
(Halmos, 1965, p.147).

Over the years various reformatory benefits of prison industry
have been suggested: enabling prisoners to support their families
(it has been announced that the Home Secretary is considering the
possibility of paying trade union rates in prison industries);
inculcating habits of work (a device first tried at Southwell in
Nottinghamshire in 1806); or simply (as a kind of occupational
therapy) combating the tedium of imprisonment. But all such suggestions have rested more on sentiment than on empirical evidence. An
examination of work in one prison produced quite opposite conclusions:

> What evidence we have gathered together casts doubt as to whether
> work is being successful in providing good work habits, skills or
> additions to the national cake....We would suggest that the maxi-
> mum economic production in the prison setting is extremely un-
> likely to be synonymous with good training, however defined, nor
> for that matter the other legitimate claims of the institution
> (ibid., p.172).

Even the claim that prison industry combats tedium may be questioned. Industrial sociologists such as Robert Blauner have analy-
sed workshop experience and pointed out that some industrial tasks
may be just complex enough to necessitate active mental involvement,
and yet not simple enough to allow for the compensation of daydream-
ing and reverie (Blauner, 1964). It is quite possible that by
making prison industry more modern and complex, tedium has been
maximized.

Although it is unnecessary here to itemize each component of the
modern prison regime and to match with objectives and evidence of
success, one could so consider agricultural and horticultural work,
inmate clubs and committees, religious provisions, psychiatric
treatment, and welfare services. In all such cases it could be
plausibly argued that there is a contribution to the physical servicing and social stability of the prison community - and thus to
the custodial objective. No substantial scientific evidence, however, could be offered indicating their furtherance of the reformatory goal.

Following a similar line of investigation and argument an American writer recently made an additional and somewhat sardonic comment:

> That is not to say that medical, psychiatric, educational and
> vocational interventions cannot or do not achieve their

objectives. Quite frequently they do so with startling effectiveness. But curing syphilis, replacing diseased teeth,
adjusting an offender to homosexuality, detoxifying an addict,
successes in teaching inmates to read or to pass high school
equivalency examination, or developing journeyman level mechani-
cal skills - these need not either individually or collectively
add up to rehabilitation, if by the latter term we imply a pattern of non-criminal behaviour. In fact we could accomplish all
of these desirable goals and turn out a more competent, more
dangerous, more sophisticated criminal, one less likely despite
his more frequent, more serious criminality to become a recidiv-
istic statistic (Sagarin and MacNamara, 1973, p.5).

At least as long ago as 1959 the Prison Commission itself pointed
to the lack of supportive evidence for the reformatory claims of
various forms of treatment. In the White Paper 'Penal Practice in a
Changing Society' (HMSO, 1959) it put forward its own analysis,
arguing that treatment could not 'in the present state of knowledge,
be given any scientific basis. It is possible to say that such and
such a percentage have not, over a given period of exposure to risk,
returned to prison. But it is not possible to say whether that
result is because of their treatment in prison, or in spite of it,
or whether it would have been the same if they had never come to
prison' (p.12). Ten years later the authorities were no more confident: 'The fact that a known proportion of discharged prisoners
are not convicted again does not of itself tell us anything about
the efficacy of the way in which they were treated in custody. We
need to estimate, for we can never know, what would have happened to
a prisoner if the court or prison system had dealt with him in some
other way...' (HMSO, 1969, p.56).

Academic and other research on the efficacy of various forms of
penal treatment has reached similar conclusions. Hood and Sparks
(1970), in a review of relevant research, found that for many offenders probation was at least as effective as an institutional sentence in preventing recidivism and (for the benefit of the sanguine)
they emphasized that the research which they cited 'cannot be interpreted as showing that probation is especially effective as a method
of treatment'. Other research showed that fines and discharges were
much more effective than either probation or imprisonment: this
held for first offenders and for recidivists of all age groups.
Further, on the basis of both British and American research, they
were able to conclude that longer institutional sentences were no
more effective than shorter ones. Supporting some treatment hopes,
Hood and Sparks cited research that indicated improvement in response to treatment of what they described as a 'medium risk' category (offenders without good chances or whose offending was not
persistent), and suggested that an examination of the relationship
between types of treatment and types of offender might yield more
productive results. Even with the latter approach, however, they
were obliged to remark on 'the generally negative results obtained'.
These observations are in general agreement with earlier findings of
Hood (1967): 'There are no substantial research results that throw
any light on the effectiveness of penalties in deterring potential
offenders', and further that 'at present treatments are more or less
equally irrelevant'.

In his stimulating Hamlyn Lectures in 1971 Professor Sir Rupert
Cross assessed penal reform over the last hundred years. He recognized the development of 'a more generous penal theory', but was
obliged none the less to confess to 'a profound scepticism about
the extent to which prison can truly be said to be reformatory'. He
remarked that 'The change of heart, acquisition of other interests,
or maturation, can, and no doubt sometimes does occur in prison;
but they are much more likely to occur outside owing for example, to
the influence of a friend, the guidance of a probation officer, membership of a sympathetic group, matrimony or change of employment.
The chances of deterioration in prison are at least as great as
those of reform' (Cross, 1971, pp.84-5).

A recent and highly competent analysis of the ideology of imprisonment in England and America by Gordon Hawkins contended that 'All
the evidence points to the conclusion that the penitentiary system
(i.e. reformatory imprisonment) was, quite literally, as it happens,
a monumental mistake' (Blom-Cooper, 1974, p.115). Further confirma-
tion of this view is given in an American survey of studies of penal
treatment programmes between 1940 and the late 1960s. Alvin Cohn
describes his results as 'devastating' - 'correctional rehabilitation does not work' (in Sagarin and MacNamara, 1973, p.50).

Although a few studies may be cited to the contrary, the over-
whelming weight of evidence points to the conclusion that it makes
little difference what form of penal treatment is applied to an
offender, since the results will be similarly indifferent. Nigel
Walker (1968) has used the phrase 'The interchangeability of penal
measures' to describe this assessment of the evidence. Such a
position may be the basis for a plea for more humane treatment.
This is Davies's contention (1974, p.161): 'if the campaigner is
arguing that there are better alternatives to imprisonment, then the
evidence is not strong; if on the other hand, he is arguing that
release into the community appears to work just as well - i.e. that
imprisonment does not itself act as a deterrent or reformative influence - then he can quote a good deal of empirical support for his
argument, as well as asserting that the alternatives are probably
cheaper.' But as Davies admits elsewhere, such a case is based on
the doubtful assumption that imprisonment is imposed primarily to
reform the individual offender. Thomas (1970) has argued that a
dual sentencing system now exists, in which the courts may apply
either the principle of individualization, or the tariff, which is
based on concepts of retribution and general deterrence. Obviously
this latter sentencing system is a formidable barrier to the whole-
sale adoption of non-custodial measures on purely cost-effective or
humanitarian grounds. The hopes of many a liberal critic of imprisonment have foundered on an inability to recognize the general
deterrent and retributive elements in the functions and sentences of
the courts.

In the light of the evidence that has increasingly become available on the efficacy of prison treatment, it is hard to say whether
the hopes of the last eighty or so years have been hubristic or
naive. Viewed in perspective, the extremely complicated phenomena
of crime and imprisonment have been treated in a cavalier and almost
arbitrary manner by policy-makers and administrators. Hall Williams
(1970, p.200) has well expressed his reaction to such grossly over-

simple approaches to penal measures: 'This is patent nonsense, for
we cannot properly speak of the success of a penal measure in isolation from the offender's total situation, including his home and
family surroundings, his employment situation, and the community in
which he lives and the degree to which he shares or is influenced by
its norms. Viewed thus, any talk of the success of a penal measure
seems slightly unrealistic.'

Before going on to ask the obvious next question - how can treatment occupy such a prominent place in the objectives and methods of
the prison system in the face of such a coherent body of hostile
evidence - I would like to examine more generally the possibility
and desirability of there being any effective form of prison treatment.

Objective limitations to the methods of prison treatment were
first discovered in the course of the elaboration of punitive regimes. Early in the nineteenth century, seeking the objective of
less-eligibility, prison administrators attempted to make the physical conditions of the imprisoned more unpleasant than those of the
poorest freeman. Immediately constraints of institutional maintenance became apparent: dietary, sanitary and other environmental
conditions could not be reduced to the level of the poor - never
mind below it - without incurring epidemics and the death of large
numbers of prisoners, making imprisonment impossible. Thus it
was discovered that institutions could not replicate the physical
environment of the poor without turning into charnel houses.
(Attempts to make the deterrent New Poor Law workhouses less eligible on a similar basis also had to be abandoned. Deterrent policy
was implemented by making institutional social conditions less
eligible.)

By the middle of the century the physical constraints upon the
design of a punitive regime were well known. Desirous of inflicting
severe and efficient punishment, administrators had to develop other
possibilities. Pentonville provides a good example of their endeavours. It was conceived of in what might crudely be described as
cathartic terms. Proclivity to wickedness would be curbed or driven
out by prolonged solitary confinement (albeit, well fed, sanitary
and warm); goodness, in the form of religion and trade-training,
could then effectively enter the life of the prisoner. But the
narrow limits of human psychological stability soon became manifest
in an intolerable incidence of insanity. So was cut short this experiment in punitive reformation, based on techniques familiar today
as isolation and sensory deprivation.

If prisoners cannot be isolated for prolonged periods without the
risk of insanity, what other punitive treatment alternatives remain?
Associated prisoners might be subjected to a variety of penal regimes; these might include, for example, rigidly enforced silence
and severe and arduous labour. Aside from the extremely tenuous
utilitarian assumptions that such treatment will affect propensity
to commit crime, all the evidence is that (and only slightly impeded
by the silence rule) an inmate culture invariably emerges in such
conditions, which provides a degree of social and physical compensation for the deprivations and pains of imprisonment. The greater
the pains and deprivation, the stronger and more necessary the
inmate culture. Even a regime which sought to punish purely

psychologically by emphasizing the stigmatization of imprisonment is likely to produce an appropriate responding counter-culture. Such social processes have been seen at work not only in prisons, but in custodial-type classroom situations, where the counter culture, besides providing social compensation, may also generate crime (Hargreaves, 1967). No prison regime can escape the physical, psychological, and social constraints inseparable from institutional living - whether methods are physically or socially punitive.

More sophisticated correctional technologies, which might be operated within the known social and physical environmental constraints, cannot offer the prison administrator any firmer promise of success. Paterson's borstal regime was in large measure designed to minimize the contamination of inmate-counter-cultures and in the inter-war years seemed to have some success in this regard. Its effect on recidivism was much more problematical. Similarly, group counselling, introduced into English prisons in the late 1950s, may well have decreased the antagonism between some staff and inmate groups and produced a more harmonious institutional atmosphere, but it cannot be shown to have affected inmates' recidivism rates. The evidence regarding all forms of group psychotherapy is similarly weak respecting claims of long-term changes in behaviour. This applies even to methods of treatment which have been described as 'brainwashing': operative conditioning, based on a system of rewards, and aversion therapy applied by means of drugs or electric shock. (1) New drugs may change the position, however. Mitford (1974) reports that anectine is being used in the United States, to induce pain and fear through sensations of drowning, in the hope of enhancing the effectiveness of aversion therapy. Other techniques reported by Mitford include sensory deprivation and 'stress assessment'. Whilst they can undoubtedly have awesomely damaging and bizarre effects, these penal therapies cannot be shown to prevent crime except, possibly, through the mental and social breakdown of their patients.

Psychiatric techniques are similarly inconclusive, in so far as assessment has been permitted at all by a group notorious for its professional reticence. (2) Stanley Cohen (1974) has probably summarized what is known of the part of psychiatry in the prison system: 'The present functions of psychiatry in prison - both here and in systems like America, Scandinavia and Holland - are obscure. Psychiatry may involve little more than a cooling-out, whereby therapy is used to help the inmate to adjust to the regime. Or else it may be consciously manipulated by the prisoner as a form of making out in the institution.' Other, more direct techniques of behaviour modification and control exist, some of which have been tried in Britain. Continuous medication has long been an important control technique in mental hospitals, and is used with certain long-term and irksome prisoners. Technically this approach has considerable potential for development: as new and powerful sedatives (some already in use in the United States) become available it will be possible to reduce 'problem' prisoners to a virtually dormant state. (3)

Incapacitation may be secured by means other than sedation; drugs which alter the structure of the mind may be used. Surgical operations may be carried out upon the brain or on other parts of

the body as, for example, the castration of certain sex offenders in
European countries. There has been at least one recent British
report of neurosurgery being used to 'reduce or abolish the aggres-
sive element in the sexual drive'. Results are said to be 'promising', though the writer laments that 'suitable cases are not easy to
find' (Blom-Cooper, 1974, p.123). Hormones (some of which might be
described as chemical castration) have also been used in Britain, on
a relatively small scale, in the field of mental health and in
prisons, in the treatment of sex offenders. Administered by various
means, including the implantation of capons, their results have been
inconclusive, and the rather horrific bodily changes, produced as a
side-effect, have provoked considerable public controversy. (4)
These forms of treatment, despite their modern trappings, have a
certain primitive character. Incapacitation has, in fact, ancient
origins and was an intended function of such retributive punishments
as the amputation of limbs, mutilation and branding.

Whilst it is doubtful that extensive use of surgical and chemical
means of 'neutralizing' offenders would be tolerated in Britain in
the present state of public and administrative opinion, it is as
well to remember that the boundary lines of propriety are not easily
drawn and are continually changing: English psychiatric technique
of the 1950s and 1960s included the extensive use of electro-convul-
sive treatment and lobotomy, even though results proved difficult to
predict. It is precisely because physiological psychology is still
relatively underdeveloped in knowledge and technique that its
response to a phenomenon as complicated as crime is of as general
a nature as incapacitation.

All the foregoing methods involve control, but the development of
electronic devices may enable control to be combined with a form of
continuous surveillance to produce a security system which, at least
theoretically, could be sufficiently efficient as to render most
prisons obsolete and unnecessary. Cohen (1974) cites a forecast of
such a development:

In the very near future, a computer technology will make possible
alternatives to imprisonment. The development of systems for
telemetering information from sensors implanted in or on the body
will soon make possible the observation and control of human behaviour without physical contact. Through such telemetric devices, it will be possible to maintain a 24 hour-a-day surveillance over the subject and to intervene electronically or physically to influence and control selected behaviour. It will thus
be possible to exercise control over human behaviour and from a
distance without physical contact. The possible implications for
criminology and corrections of such telemetric systems is tremen-
dously significant.

This latter instance introduces what I think is the most important
consideration in the limitations of treatment. Let us suppose that
in the field of group therapy, aversion therapy or operant conditioning, or in surgical, psychiatric, chemical or electronic techniques,
problems were overcome, and reliable and relatively precise means of
modifying and controlling behaviour were developed. How should we
react to such discoveries and innovations? From one point of view
they could be seen as a boon - a valuable and socially beneficial
means of replacing punishment by diagnostic treatment. Prisons

might in large part become redundant; the advice of social scien-
tists and doctors might thus, at last, achieve the same status as
the advice given by engineers and chemists to industrialists; the
treatment of crime could, in time, be reduced to a series of routine
tables and treatments administered by technicians. The potential
humanitarian advantages of such developments should not be under-
estimated: prison officials whose futile duty it is repeatedly to
lock up obsessive offenders for long periods, would surely be among
the first to welcome the humane benefits of scientific therapy.

But a contrary view may be more persuasive. The sociologist
Emile Durkheim and others have suggested that crime is necessary and
functional for society; it serves continually to distinguish the
legitimate from the illegitimate, and by the social stigmatization
of offenders provides identity and reward for those who keep the
law. Moreover the level of crime can be seen as an index to the
degree of social control exercised at any given time. Societies
with low crime-rates are likely to be heavily controlled, closed
and non-innovatory. These observations help to emphasize what
might be described as the 'positive' aspects of crime - crime as a
cost of other social conditions and phenomena which are thought
desirable. In the same way it may be argued that the prison population is an index of the level of individual freedom in a society
at any given time; and an excessively small population may be as
indicative of a repressive society as much as one which is very
large.   The necessity for society to incarcerate offenders, sometimes for long periods, is a testament to the degree of behavioural
autonomy which man still strives for and possesses - even in industrial society. Could there ever be sufficient safeguards acceptably
to give to an administration the effective means directly to modify
and control behaviour, even in the interests of the curtailment of
crime? If technical developments make this futuristic dilemma an
issue of policy, its resolution will require consideration not only
of secondary questions such as efficiency and safety, but also basic
constitutional, political, and legal values.

In the light of this catalogue of objections to efficacious penal
treatment it is now time to return to the earlier question, and to
ask why treatment continues to occupy a prominent position in the
rhetoric of the modern prison system. First, it is necessary to
distinguish between theory and practice; theory may usefully, as an
example, be taken to refer to the prison rules. Rule 1 states 'The
purpose of the training and treatment of convicted prisoners shall
be to encourage and assist them to lead a good and useful life.'
Yet, in practice, as we have seen, the Prison Department (at least
at senior policy making and administrative levels) has acknowledged
that there exists no sound means for the attainment of this objective; the studied absence of discussion of effective treatment in
successive annual reports confirms this acknowledgment. Indeed,
recognition of the interchangeability of penal measures has severely
undermined the separate existence and function of what might be
termed traditional treatment institutions. Amendments to rules have
narrowed the differences between specialist milieu treatment establishments such as borstals and detention centres, and prisons in
general (HMSO 1972, pp.32-3). (5) However, the Prison Department,
even whilst accepting that current expectations of efficacious

treatment must remain low, has hopes for the future: 'research may
...suggest new and better forms of treatment, and any that are promising must be tried out and evaluated' (HMSO, 1969, p.56). Second,
the Prison Department distinguishes quite clearly between the purpose of training and treatment as expressed in the prison rules and
the broader functions of prisons. 'People in Prison' expressed this
distinction:

> First it is the task of the service, under the law, to hold those
> committed to custody and to provide conditions for their deten-
> tion which are currently acceptable to society. Second, in deal-
> ing with convicted offenders, there is an obligation on the ser-
> vice to do all that may be possible within the currency of the
> sentence 'to encourage and assist them to lead a good and useful
> life' (HMSO, 1969, p.7).

Official understanding, then, is that the custodial objective is
primary, and such treatment as is possible within that context occu-
pies the next place in the hierarchy of objectives.

Part of the explanation for the persistence of the treatment goal
and the associated rhetoric arises from the history of English
prisons. From the time of Howard reformers have consistently used
the banner of treatment in their efforts to regulate and ameliorate
prison conditions.   Early reformers sought to justify the innovation of paid officials and purpose-built sanitary accommodation
to sceptical or indifferent justices on the grounds that the reformation of criminals would eventually compensate for the initial out-
lay of funds. Not only would the corruption of young and first-time
offenders cease, it was claimed, but the habitual criminal would be
reformed.

Treatment, it has been argued, has two distinct branches -
punishment and rehabilitation. In the course of the evolution of
the prison system attempts have been made to combine the two elements - as at Pentonville in the early years. Generally, although
both forms of treatment have been used together, one or the other
has been obviously pre-eminent. This was the case at Reading gaol
between the 1840s and 1860s, where the regime placed greater stress
on education and religion. By contrast, in most gaols in the period
following the Carnarvon Committee of 1863, treatment became far more
punitive. Nor was this merely by a desire for retribution; penal
reformers such as William Tallack, Secretary of the Howard Association from 1866 to 1901, strongly supported the punitive separate
confinement discipline which was the basis of the Du Cane system because of their belief in its reformatory ability (Rose, 1961, Chapter
2).

At the turn of the nineteenth and twentieth centuries, the balance in treatment began to shift yet again - from punishment to rehabilitative training. But whereas critics such as Hobhouse and
Brockway (1922) opposed punitive treatment because of its irrational
basis and inefficiency, the training methods which they wished to
substitute in its place were supported by no more evidence or experience. This was part of the politics of the situation: to induce
a change in policy the reformers were obliged to claim greater efficiency for their proposals. It is likely, however, that the reformers' recommendations were more influenced by their humanitarian
sentiments - their abhorrence of unnecessary human suffering - than

by the analytical methods which they so wholeheartedly and critically applied to punitive imprisonment.

For the last fifty years this basic contradiction in the posture
of reformers has remained. It is true that some critics have emphasized the need for alternatives to imprisonment (often making
unsubstantiated claims for the efficacy of non-custodial measures).
But for the majority - those reformers who accepted as necessary
the continued existence of the prison system - proposals for ameli-
orations in conditions have rarely been put forward on explicitly
humanitarian grounds alone. Usually it has been argued that changes
in conditions would more effectively meet the official objectives of
imprisonment.

And so a clearly defined convention has emerged, in which 'reform'
has become associated with an extension of rehabilitative training
facilities, and 'reaction' with a resistance to such changes. It
has become difficult to criticize reformatory treatment and training
without incurring accusations that such questioning strengthens the
hand of 'reactionaries'. Roger Hood (1974, p.1) has recently made
this point in his criticism of indeterminate sentences: 'Such a
system of "indeterminate" sentencing has been a part of the reformers' platform for so many years and the arguments against it have
been so readily dismissed as "reactionary" or "retributive" in the
worst senses of these pejorative terms, that few in this country
have thought to raise them.'

So though the method by which both the 'reactionaries' and 'reformers' have arrived at their respective penal nostrums has been
irrational, the training approach has appealed to many as being more
acceptable in terms of content: it has not required the infliction
of unnecessary pain. Thus it could be argued that the treatment
objective and methods have remained largely unchallenged because
they have been seen as the lesser of two evils. This unwillingness
to criticize rehabilitative goals whilst conducting a polemic
against punitive and retributive treatment has required calculated
inconsistency in the application of the scientific method, almost
amounting to double-think.

Cohen (1974) has argued that 'Prison reformers have fallen too
easily for the rhetoric of therapy (instead of treating it with
caution, and facing the unpalatable consequences of recognising the
prison for what it is). They have been lured by notions such as the
therapeutic community into thinking that the same sacrifices can
serve the gods of both punishment and treatment.' (6)

On their part, administrators and policy-makers have responded to
repeated failures in their methods not by questioning the feasibility of reformatory goals, but by renewed searching for other and more
efficient techniques; alternatively they claimed that better facilities were required in order fully to apply the reformatory methods.
By shifting the focus of criticism from the feasibility of objectives and the rationality of methods, to factors such as buildings,
equipment, and staff, it must have seemed as though judgment could
be postponed almost indefinitely.

A further aspect of this collusion of liberal reformers and administrators has been the diffusion of the concepts and terminology
of the social sciences. Because of the professional division of
labour, notions put forward tentatively (or indeed dogmatically) in

an academic environment have been applied by administrators in an
organizational setting with an unwarranted confidence in their
practical effects. Given the bureaucratic and hierarchical nature
of prison organization, such imported concepts have acquired all the
authority of their superordinate sponsors. An examination of this
process might well reveal it to be a strong contributory factor in
the changes in treatment 'fashions' in the prison system which have
been so marked over the last few decades. It might also be associated with the cynical and manipulative attitude of subordinate staff,
who often informally describe the official goals and methods as inappropriate and unattainable; but who, individually, must embrace
them as part of their duties and in pursuit of career advancement.

However, the historical development and circumstances of prison
reform and administration do not by themselves provide sufficient
explanation for the present high place given to rehabilitative objectives and methods. It cannot be said, for example, that the
Prison Department has positively concealed the flimsy nature of the
evidence supporting its reformatory policy. Nor can it be argued
that reformatory training has recently been necessary to resist a
pressing case for retributive and deterrent punishment. What difficulties might arise if reformatory treatment and training were
explicitly and fully abandoned by the Prison Department?

There would first, be a problem in public relations. It is
likely that public opinion is substantially retributive and punitive. Many members of the public, for instance, would probably
find conditions in training prisons and borstals excessively com-
fortable and lax. Popular expectations of imprisonment are still
conditioned by convict cartoons complete with broad arrows and
cropped hair. What reaction would there be, then, to a penal institution designed only to ensure humane containment? Some indi-
cation that this would be impatient and intolerant has been given by
the response to conditions in the 'E-wing' at Durham prison in the
late 1960s, when an approximately similar objective was stated
(Cohen and Taylor, 1972). The political disadvantages of abandoning
treatment claims are not, however, crucial. Policy-change is never
so simple a matter as discovering and acting upon 'the truth'.
There is no reason to suppose that abandonment of treatment and
training need formally be marked by anything more than the down-
grading and omission noticeable in the Prison Department reports
over the last several years. Internal departmental interpretation
of policy would be the crucial element.

A more difficult consideration in policy change could be staff
motivation and morale: would a policy change not adversely affect
the recruitment of suitable staff at all levels, but particularly
the governor grades? What kind of person could be found to undertake a task redefined more to resemble the work of a warehouseman
than that of a therapist? The social-work reference group, which
has been a potent support for many prison staff, would seemingly
cease to be relevant. (7) Further, the rehabilitative ideology has
always required and legitimized the humane treatment of inmates by
officer grade staff: what would happen if it were to be removed?

Possible answers to the foregoing questions might best be given
by examining more closely the implications of a 'humane containment'
policy. This would necessarily require commitment to a 'least-

damage' objective, i.e. the system would have to seek to ensure that
a prisoner was damaged by the experience of incarceration to the
least possible extent. Efforts would therefore have to be directed
to the avoidance of physical and psychic deterioration; to offer
suitable prison employment; to maintain (or maybe even to procure)
the necessary family links and variety of connections with the outside community. These objectives would involve considerable problems of management and administration, and a reorganization of certain social work agencies. But to offset the drawbacks to some
extent it is possible that some subordinate staff cynicism, which
produces withdrawal and minimum co-operation, would be diminished,
yielding desirable organizational benefits. (8) Similar advantages
may well accrue for staff-inmate relations. The physical and social
environment of prison should be greatly improved, and the bitterness
that largely baseless training claims seem to engender in inmates
would be avoided.

A similar case has recently been closely argued by Norval
Morris. In a complex consideration of issues of jurisprudence and
sentencing Morris recognizes the unviable nature of most claims for
prison treatment - 'what it all comes to is this: prison behaviour
is not a predictor of community behaviour.'

However, from that point Morris develops his critique of policy
rather differently. He places great emphasis on the non-voluntaris-
tic nature of prison training, and sees this as the chief barrier to
success. Psychological treatment requires the co-operation of the
patient, and in this respect the confusion with physical medicine is
misleading. 'We must abandon the model of physical medicine as a
guide. Education, vocational training, counselling and group therapy should continue to be provided but on an entirely voluntary
basis. There should be no suggestion that a prisoner's release may
be accelerated because of participation in such programs nor that it
might be delayed or postponed because of failure to participate....
The approach adopted should be in no way coercive but simply facili-
tative' (Morris, 1974, pp.16-8). Morris is led, moreover, to recom-
mend the establishment of a treatment establishment within a custodial prison system. This prison would cater exclusively for volunteers, mainly from among the more dangerous and violent inmates.

Although fraught with difficulties, theoretical and practical,
this notion deserves further study. At the very least it might
enable the politically and morally significant concept of volunta-
ristic treatment to be tested under optimum conditions, and could
preserve an important element of diversity in the prison system.

By embracing more fully the policy of humane containment the
Prison Department would not, therefore, be faced with the withdrawal of welfare, recreational and industrial facilities from
prisons. Rather, these facilities would be seen to have a more
legitimate function and they would be entrusted with more attainable objectives. Containment with minimum damage would obviously
need careful definition and operationalization, but it presents
fewer problems in this respect than rehabilitation. Measurement
and assessment should be easier and the various provisions and
procedures could frequently be questioned and tested, and modified
as required. It would appear that a new policy emphasis would
ultimately require extensive changes in buildings and facilities.

Staff tasks and working conditions would expand and improve, becoming more demanding, requiring greater skills and offering a
greater range of intrinsic satisfactions. Much more work outside
the prison even on the part of basic grade officers, for example,
might be required.

Rehabilitative imprisonment has had a tyrannical aspect. In the
first instance it underpinned the 'closed shop' of permissible reformatory criticisms. The fear of showing one's flanks to the
'reactionaries' (irrational though it is) could be put aside, and a
more constructive and vigorous style of criticism and evaluation
could develop. The benefits of this over a number of years could
well be inestimable. Certainly critical evaluation faces a major
task in the exposure of the pseudo-scientific ideology of 'corrections'.

Within prisons the protective ambiguities of the two-part definition of treatment would be shattered; it would no longer be possible for administrators to claim credence for the view that 'We
need a view of treatment that embraces all that is done by or for
the offender in custody.' The circular justification of prison
treatment would be ruptured, and the old question and answer routine
- What is treatment? All that happends in prison. What happens in
prison? Treatment. What is treatment? etc. etc. would of necessity
have to be abandoned. In short, it would become extremely difficult
to use the supposedly inseparable relationship of institutional
maintenance and individual treatment to justify practices which were
supported by nothing more than administrative convenience or bureaucratic caution.

An examination of perhaps the greatest benefit of a change in
policy lies outside the scope of this article and this book; I
refer to the consequent changes in sentencing policy. The aims of
sentencing are complex, and include deterrence, the protection of
society, retribution and the reformation of the offender. If imprisonment ceased to be recognized as an effective means of securing
the latter objective, many offenders who are now sent to prison and,
more particularly, borstal, ostensibly for reformatory reasons,
could no longer legitimately be so sentenced.

Prisons would retain their deterrent function - both general and
individual - through what in effect would be a confiscation of certain liberties and time. (9) Society could continue to protect
itself by securely confining dangerous offenders; those who would
not merit close custody being sent to less-secure or open establishments. The retributive function would still be accomplished,
and experiment with reparation would be facilitated by the greater
flexibility of a purely custodial regime.

Stanley Cohen (1974) has painted a less hopeful picture of custodial imprisonment. His argument is that the reformatory endeavours
of governments, administrations and voluntary bodies have increasingly restricted the categories of people sent to prison. Demands
for retribution and deterrence will ensure the existence of a resi-
dual group thought appropriate for imprisonment:

Paradoxically, because of the liberals' success, this whole group
will be defined in even more negative and destructive terms.
They will be the hard core, the bottom of the barrel, the recal-
citrants, the incorrigibles: those for whom one can do nothing

more than shut away in dispersal prisons, or security wings, and
now control units. Prisons for this group of offenders are des-
tined to become human warehouses: places where people are stored
until society can think of something else to do with them.
In the immediate future Cohen predicts the emergence of two types of
prisons: the human warehouses or purely custodial prisons for the
incorrigibles, and more advanced quasi-rehabilitative prisons for
other offenders.

I find this picture overdrawn, though its caution may well be
healthy. Recent political and pressure-group response to the use of
'control units' for extremely difficult and subversive prisoners has
shown that in Britain the logic of segregation will be heavily circumscribed by public anxiety. It is possible greatly to overesti-
mate the number of 'incorrigibles' in the prison system and the
degree to which they form an identifiable group. For example, we
still know relatively little about the extent of 'professional'
crime for which long determinate sentences might be expected, and
most life sentences are imposed for domestic murders. Moreover, it
is doubtful if the penal system will ever develop to the point where
imprisonment even approximates to the institutional segregation of
hopeless cases only. Many periodic offenders, particularly young
males, will need to be held in custody as a control measure;
indeed the current agitation by some magistrates for the provision
of secure institutions for children indicates that a fairly wide
range of offenders will continue to be incarcerated. Such offenders
will, in the vast majority of cases, simply grow out of their behavioural difficulties, and the need for imprisonment. In any event,
it would be foolish to assume that the present trend to non-custodial measures is irreversible.

Nevertheless, Cohen's contention that 'incorrigibles' will be
controlled according to the logic of segregation is plausible. Such
sifting of recalcitrant prisoners into smaller and smaller units has
always been a basic control technique, even when the sanction of
corporal punishment was available. New control problems are likely
to be presented by the relatively small number of extremely long
sentence prisoners that have begun to accumulate in the system, and
who may have to be detained for all or most of their natural lives.
In their case purely custodial imprisonment within as liberal a
regime as is compatible with security requirements seems to be un-
avoidable: 'treatment' simply would not make sense for such
prisoners.

Obviously the full implications of policy change require more
extensive examination; many problems (and benefits) would become
apparent only in the course of time and practice. But it is not
necessary to justify change to a policy, in order to support the
case for a change from a policy. The history of English prisons
since the end of the eighteenth century has been largely a history
of the failure of attempts to procure effective forms of behaviour
change. Any future technical developments that would break with
that history would pose such a threat to political and civic liberties as to merit the most strenuous opposition. The continued use
of imprisonment is a symbol that certain basic rights are still
protected from the benevolent threat of technical efficiency and
administrative power. Imprisonment is a price, but it is a price

that the community might be well advised to continue to pay. Hopefully, the policy of treatment and training has reached the end of the road, which in retrospect can be seen always to have been a cul-de-sac.

NOTES

1 An uncritical account of the former - described as 'contingency management - is given in Sagarin and MacNamara (1973, chapter 5). Despite its manifold flaws the British system has been sceptical of theory-based disciplinary systems, and has preferred a more piecemeal and pragmatic approach. Against this background, and at a time of crisis for the treatment model it is surprising to hear, therefore, that a mild version of operative conditioning is to be tried at Glen Parva Borstal. The regime there will be partly based on 'contingency contracts' negotiated between staff and inmates. This experiment seems compatible with the drift of policy only if (A) 'treatment' continues to be officially approved for juveniles and/or (B) the basic intention of the new system is to design a more effective means of institutional control - especially needed with volatile young offenders.

2 Richard Arens, for example, in his study of insanity defence in the District of Columbia has convincingly shown that psychiatrists, relying on the protection of their profession and their standing as expert witnesses, seriously undermined the judicial process and adversely affected individual rights and liberties. Control of such powerful occupational groups poses considerable problems for the administration of criminal justice (Arens, 1974).

3 Mitford (1974, pp.129-30) cites manufacturers' reports on the possible side effects of the widely-used tranquillizer Prolixin - 'The induction of a "catatonic-like state", nausea, loss of appetite, headache, constipation, blurred vision, glaucoma, bladder paralysis, impotency, liver damage, hypertension severe enough to cause fatal cardiac arrest and cerebral endema.'

4 Quite unappreciated by some prison medical staff. R.R. Prewer, a Principal Medical Officer, for example, discusses the technique in a purely technical manner: 'It is not pretended that a hormone implant is a cure for sexual deviation - indeed, it throws out the sexual baby with the deviant bath-water; but it has proved a very effective way of keeping such offenders out of mischief. Unfortunately, many sex offenders will not accept this form of treatment, probably because it is so efficacious; others commence it and then fail to come back for replacements when once they have obtained their liberty. There is reason to believe that even more useful drugs will shortly become available for this purpose' (Blom-Cooper, 1974, p.122). I find this moral naivity alarming.

5 If the May 1974 recommendations of the Advisory Council on the Penal System on the treatment of the young adult offender are implemented, formal administrative differences between young prisoner establishments, borstals and detention centres would virtually cease. There would no longer be separate sentencing of offenders to these institutions.

6   It is only fair to add, however, that one group of penal refor-
    mers has taken a radically different path and an increasingly
    vociferous abolitionist lobby has emerged in the last few years.
    This has mainly been based in the United States. The abolition-
    ist case has been vigorously presented in publications such as
    the American Friends Service Committee's 'Struggle for Justice',
    and Jessica Mitford's 'Kind and Usual Punishment'. Such views
    are still in a minority among British penal reformers - even in
    the more radical pressure groups.

7   'The Times' (24 April 1975) cites surveys which have shown 'that
    more than three-fifths of prison officers regard themselves as
    more like probation officers than like policemen.' Norman Jepson
    (chapter 2 in this book) confirms the importance of the social-
    work reference group.

8   The Prison Officers' Association has, over recent years, expres-
    sed a desire for the more active involvement of its members in
    treatment and training tasks, as opposed to the merely custodial
    side of imprisonment. It may well welcome the facilitative tasks
    required by 'humane containment'.

9   Though it seems inevitable that the deterrent claims of imprison-
    ment may in time also be totally or partially rejected. Inter-
    esting and useful preliminary investigations were recently
    reported in a 'New Society' article by Baxter and Nuttall (1975),
    and some key issues have been taken up by Sir Brian MacKenna (a
    senior judge) in his essay General Deterrence (in Blom-Cooper,
    1974, chapter 14).

REFERENCES

AMERICAN FRIENDS SERVICE COMMITTEE (1971), 'Struggle for Justice:
A Report on Crime and Punishment in America', New York, Hill & Wang.
ARENS, RICHARD (1974), 'Insanity Defence', Philosophical Library,
New York.
BAXTER, ROBERT and NUTTALL, CHRIS (1975), Severe Sentences: No
Deterrent to Crime?, 'New Society', no.639, 2 January.
BLAUNER, ROBERT (1964), 'Alienation and Freedom', University of
Chicago Press.
BLOM-COOPER, LOUIS (ed.) (1974), 'Progress in Penal Reform', Oxford
University Press.
COHEN, STANLEY (1974), Human Warehouses: the Future of our Prisons?,
'New Society', no.632, 14 November.
COHEN, STANLEY and TAYLOR, LAURIE (1972), 'Psychological Survival',
Penguin.
CROSS, RUPERT (1971), 'Punishment, Prison and the Public', Stevens.
DAVIES, MARTIN (1974), 'Prisoners of Society', Routledge & Kegan
Paul.
HALMOS, PAUL (ed.) (1965), 'Sociological Review. Monograph No.9',
University of Keele.
HARGREAVES, DAVID (1967), 'Social Relations in a Secondary School',
Routledge & Kegan Paul.
HMSO (1959), 'Penal Practice in a Changing Society', Cmnd 645.
HMSO (1960), 'Report of the Commissioners for Prisons for 1959,
Cmnd 1117.

HMSO (1964), 'Prison Rules', Statutory Instrument No.388.
HMSO (1965), 'The Adult Offender', Cmnd 2852.
HMSO (1967), 'Report on the Work of the Prison Department, 1966',
Cmnd 3408.
HMSO (1969), 'People in Prison', Cmnd 4214.
HMSO (1973), 'Report on the Work of the Prison Department, 1972',
Cmnd 5375.
HMSO (1974), 'Report on the Work of the Prison Department, 1973',
Cmnd 5767.
HOBHOUSE, STEPHEN and BROCKWAY, A. FENNER (1922), 'English Prisons
Today', Longmans.
HOOD, ROGER and SPARKS, RICHARD (1970), 'Key Issues in Criminology',
Weidenfeld & Nicolson.
HOOD, ROGER (1967), Research on the Effectiveness of Punishments and
Treatments, 'Collected Studies in Criminological Research', Council
of Europe.
HOOD, ROGER (1974), 'Tolerance and the Tariff', NACRO Papers and
Reprints.
MITFORD, JESSICA (1974), 'The American Prison Business', Allen &
Unwin.
MORRIS, NORVAL (1974), 'The Future of Imprisonment', University of
Chicago Press.
ROSE, GORDON (1961), 'The Struggle for Penal Reform', Stevens.
SAGARIN, EDWARD and MACNAMARA, DONAL E.J. (eds) (1973), 'Rehabili-
tation', Praeger.
THOMAS, D.A. (1970), 'Principles of Sentencing', Heinemann.
WALKER, NIGEL (1968), 'Crime and Punishment in Britain', Edinburgh
University Press.
WILLIAMS, J.E. HALL (1970), 'The English Penal System in Transition',
Butterworth.

SUGGESTED FURTHER READING

1 PRISON HISTORY

BABINGTON, ANTHONY, 'The English Bastile', MacDonald, 1971.
BLOM-COOPER, LOUIS (ed.), 'Progress in Penal Reform', Oxford University Press, 1974.
CLAY, W.L., 'The Prison Chaplain', Macmillan, 1861.
CROSS, RUPERT, 'Punishment, Prison and the Public', Stevens, 1971.
FOX, LIONEL W., 'The English Prison and Borstal Systems', Routledge & Kegan Paul, 1952.
GRUNHUT, MAX, 'Penal Reform', Oxford University Press, 1948.
HINDE, R.S.E., 'The British Penal System 1773-1950', 1951.
HOOD, ROGER, 'Borstal Reassessed', Heinemann, 1965.
HOWARD, D.L., 'John Howard: Prison Reformer', C. Johnson, 1958.
HOWARD, D.L., 'The English Prisons', Methuen, 1960.
IVE, GEORGE, 'A History of Penal Methods', S. Paul, 1914.
JOHNSON, W. BRANCH, 'The English Prison Hulks', Phillamore, 1970.
MAYHEW, H. and BINNY, J., 'Criminal Prisons of London', Griffin, 1862.
PLAYFAIR, GILES, 'The Punitive Obsession', Gollancz, 1971.
PUGH, RALPH B., 'Imprisonment in Medieval England', Cambridge University Press, 1968.
RADZINOWICZ, LEON, 'A History of English Criminal Law', Stevens, 4 vols, 1948-68.
ROSE, GORDON, 'The Struggle for Penal Reform', Stevens, 1961.
ROTHMAN, DAVID J., 'The Discovery of the Asylum', Little, Brown & Company, 1971.
SHAW, A.G.L., 'Convicts and the Colonies', Faber, 1966.
THOMAS, J.E., 'The English Prison Officer Since 1850', Routledge & Kegan Paul, 1971.
TOBIAS, J.J., 'Prince of Fences', Valentine, Mitchell, 1974.
WEBB, SIDNEY and WEBB, BEATRICE, 'English Prisons Under Local Government', Cass, 1963.
WRIGHT, MARTIN (ed.), 'Use of Criminology Literature', Butterworth, 1974.

Official Publications

'House of Lords Select Committee in the State of the Gaols and
Houses of Correction', 1835
Annual Reports of the Inspectors of Prison, Directors of Convict
Prisons and Commissioners of Prisons (1836-1963).
'Report from Select Committee of House of Lords on the Present State
of Discipline in Gaols and Houses of Correction' (Carnarvon Commit-
tee), 1863.
'Report of the Departmental Committee on Prisons' (Gladstone Commit-
tee), 1895, HMSO, Cmnd 7702.
'Minutes of Evidence taken by the Departmental Committee on Prisons',
(Gladstone Committee), 1895, HMSO, Cmnd 7702-1.
'Report on the Circumstances Connected with the Recent Disorder at
Dartmoor Convict Prison' (Du Parcq Report), 1932, HMSO, Cmnd 4010.

2   CONTEMPORARY IMPRISONMENT

BLOM-COOPER, LOUIS (ed.), 'Progress in Penal Reform', Oxford Univer-
sity Press, 1974.
BOTTOMS A.E. and MCCLINTOCK, F.H., 'Criminals Coming of Age',
Heinemann, 1973.
BRIGGS, DENNIE, 'In Place of Prison', Temple Smith, 1975.
BRITISH INSTITUTE OF HUMAN RIGHTS, 'Detention: Minimum Standards of
Treatment', Barry Rose, Chichester and London, 1975.
CLEMMER, DONALD, 'The Prison Community', Holt Rinehart & Winston,
New York and London, 1940.
COHEN, STANLEY and TAYLOR, LAURIE, 'Psychological Survival', Penguin,
1972.
DAVIES, MARTIN, 'Prisoners of Society', Routledge & Kegan Paul,
1974.
EMERY, F.E., 'Freedom and Justice within Walls', Tavistock, 1970.
HALMOS, P. (ed.), 'Sociological Studies in the British Penal Ser-
vices', Sociological Review Monograph no.9, Keele, 1965.
JELLICOE, THE RT HON. THE EARL (Chairman), 'Boards of Visitors of
Penal Institutions', Report of a Committee set up by Justice, The
Howard League for Penal Reform and The National Association for the
Care and Resettlement of Offenders, Barry Rose, Chichester and
London, 1975.
KLARE, HUGH J., 'People in Prison', Pitman, 1974.
MITFORD, JESSICA, 'The American Prison Business', Allen & Unwin,
1974.
MORRIS, NORVAL, 'The Future of Imprisonment', University of Chicago
Press, 1974.
MORRIS, PAULINE, 'Prisoners and their Families', Allen & Unwin,
1965.
MORRIS, T.P. and MORRIS, P.M., 'Pentonville', Routledge & Kegan
Paul, 1963.
SPARKS, RICHARD F., 'Local Prisons: The Crisis in the English Penal
System', Heinemann, 1971.
STUMPHANZER, J.S., 'Behaviour Therapy with Delinquents', Charles C.
Thomas, Springfield, Ill., 1973.
SYKES, GRESHAM M., 'The Society of Captives', Princeton University
Press, 1958.

WALKER, NIGEL, 'Crime and Punishment in Britain', Edinburgh University Press, 1968.
WALTERS, RICHARD H., 'Punishment', Penguin, 1972.
WILLIAMS, J.E. HALL, 'The English Penal System in Transition', Butterworth, 1970.
WILLIAMS, J.E. HALL, 'Changing Prisons', Peter Owen, 1975.

Official Publications

Eleventh Report of the Estimates Committee, 'Prisons, Borstals and Detention Centres', 1966-7, HCP 599.
'Report of the Inquiry into Prison Escapes and Security by Admiral of the Fleet, Earl Mountbatten of Burma',(Mountbatten Report), HMSO, 1966, Cmnd 3175.
HOME OFFICE, 'Report of the Advisory Council on the Penal System on the Regime for Long-term Prisoners in Conditions of Maximum Security', (Radzinowicz Report), HMSO, 1968.
HOME OFFICE, 'People in Prison', HMSO, 1969, Cmnd 4214.
HOME OFFICE, 'Report of the Advisory Council on the Penal System on Young Adult Offenders', (Younger Report), HMSO, 1974.
HOME OFFICE, 'Report on the Work of the Prison Department', HMSO, (annually in two parts).

JOURNALS

'British Journal of Criminology'
'Howard Journal'
'New Society'
'Prison Service Journal', HMSO.